"I am grateful for books as brief and artful as Calvin Tomkins' portrait of Gerald and Sara Murphy....I like this book particularly because it seems to say a good deal about the nature of friendship, as well as the good life, and it seems to invite our thoughts as well."
—*Newsweek*

"Tomkins' clear, gifted prose rises at times to an almost hymnal cadence....He catches the babble of some original tongues and the texture of a reverberant and fertile world as irrecoverable now as Atlantis."
—STEVEN M.L. ARONSON, *Washington Post*

"Gerald...would have been delighted by Tomkins' book. A marvel of taste and economy, it manages to convey the originality and grace of the Murphys' life."
—*Time*

"The past has a way of fading into unexpected patterns as old photographs fade, and certain figures—not always or even commonly the most famous—seem, in retrospect, to dominate these chance designs. Gerald Murphy is gradually becoming such a figure in the remembered Twenties and it is the great achievement of Cal's book that it shows both how and why."
—ARCHIBALD MACLEISH

"A lovely, lovely work of literature....You must read it."
—*Boston Globe*

belisk

ALSO BY CALVIN TOMKINS

*Merchants and Masterpieces: The Story of the
Metropolitan Museum of Art*

Eric Hoffer: An American Odyssey

The World of Marcel Duchamp

The Lewis and Clark Trail

The Bride and the Bachelors

Intermission (Novel)

LIVING WELL

IS THE BEST REVENGE

by CALVIN TOMKINS

A Dutton **Obelisk** Paperback

E. P. DUTTON | NEW YORK

This paperback edition of Living Well is the Best Revenge *first published in 1982 by E. P. Dutton.*

Most of the text appeared in The New Yorker *in somewhat different form.*

The author wishes to thank Archibald MacLeish for permission to use an excerpt from "American Letter, for Gerald Murphy," and Frances Scott Fitzgerald Smith for permission to use a letter to Sara Murphy by F. Scott Fitzgerald.

The photographs on pages 56, 60, 61, 62, and 63 are by courtesy of the estate of Cole Porter.

Published in the United States by
E. P. Dutton, Inc., 2 Park Avenue, New York, N.Y. 10016

Library of Congress Catalog Card Number: 82-72078

ISBN: 0-525-48023-4

Published simultaneously in Canada by
Clarke, Irwin & Company Limited, Toronto and Vancouver

10 9 8 7 6 5 4 3 2

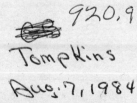

920.9
Tompkins
Aug. 7, 1984

THIS IS JUDY'S BOOK

CONTENTS

TWO FAMILIES

Even though it happened in France, it was all somehow an American experience.

—GERALD MURPHY

A writer like F. Scott Fitzgerald, whose life has always attracted more attention than his work, may have to wait a long time before his literary reputation finds its true level. The legendary quality of the Fitzgerald saga still dazzles and intrudes; we search the novels for clues to the celebrated life that has become, through various tellings and retellings, a kind of nineteen-twenties morality drama, a tragedy of squandered talent. The novel in which Fitzgerald attempted to deal more or less directly with his own tragedy, *Tender Is the Night*, has nevertheless been assuming over the years something like the status of an American classic. The book, which was generally considered a failure when it first appeared (even by Fitzgerald, who tried to improve its standing by writing a revised version that nearly everyone agreed was not as good as the

3

original) and which had gone out of print when the author died in 1940, has now become required reading in any number of modern literature courses. If many critics still regard it as a failure, they now tend to see it as a noble failure, a flawed masterpiece; and if they still complain that the disintegration of Dick Diver, its psychiatrist hero, is never satisfactorily resolved, most of them concede that Diver is one of those rare heroes in American fiction about whom the reader cares deeply and that the account of his disintegration, ambiguous though it may be, is so harrowing that it makes the glittering perfection of plot in a novel like *The Great Gatsby* seem by comparison almost too neat.

The real trouble with the book, as every college English major knows, is that Fitzgerald started out by using a friend of his named Gerald Murphy as the model for Dick Diver and then allowed Diver to change, midway through the narrative, into F. Scott Fitzgerald. To a lesser degree, he did the same thing with his heroine, Nicole Diver, who has some of the physical characteristics and mannerisms of Sara Murphy, Gerald's wife, but is in all other respects Zelda Fitzgerald. The double metamorphosis was readily apparent at the time to friends of the Fitzgeralds and the Murphys. Ernest Hemingway wrote Fitzgerald a cutting letter about the book, accusing him of cheating with his material; by starting with the Murphys and then changing them into different people, Hemingway contended, Fitzgerald had produced not people at all but beautifully faked case histories. Gerald Murphy raised the same point when he read the novel, and Fitzgerald's reply nearly floored him. "The book," Fitzgerald said, "was inspired by Sara and you, and the way I feel about you both and the way you live, and the last part of it is Zelda and me because you and Sara are the same people as Zelda and me." This astonishing statement served to confirm a long-held conviction of Sara Murphy's that Fitzgerald knew very little about people and nothing at all about the Murphys.

When *Tender Is the Night* came out in 1934, after many delays, the lives of these four friends no longer bore much resemblance to the lives of their fictional counterparts. The Murphys had left Europe, where they were living when Fitzgerald met them. Gerald Murphy was to spend the next twenty-two years in his father's old position as president of Mark Cross, the New York leather-goods store, a position he took out of necessity and from which he retired, with relief, in 1956. Neither of the Murphys particularly enjoyed reading the novel that Fitzgerald had dedicated "To Gerald and Sara—Many Fêtes." Sara, who was rather offended by it, said once that she rejected categorically "any resemblance to us or to anyone we knew at any time." Gerald admired the quality of the writing and the emotional depth of certain passages, but the book as a whole did not seem successful to him. Years later, on rereading it, he was fascinated to discover (he had not noticed it the first time) how many details Fitzgerald had drawn from life during the years the two couples spent together in Paris and on the Riviera—the years from 1924 to 1929. Almost every incident, he became aware, almost every conversation in the opening section of the book had some basis in an actual event or conversation involving the Murphys, although it was often altered or distorted in detail.

"When I like men," Fitzgerald once wrote, "I want to be like them—I want to lose the outer qualities that give me my individuality and be like them." Fitzgerald wanted to be like Gerald Murphy because he admired Murphy as much as any man he had ever met and because he was thoroughly fascinated, and sometimes thoroughly baffled, by the life the Murphys had created for themselves and their friends. It was a life of great originality and considerable beauty, and some of its special quality comes through in the first hundred pages of *Tender Is the Night.* In the eyes of the young actress Rosemary Hoyt, the Divers represented "the exact furthermost evolution of a class, so that most people seemed awkward beside them." Dick Diver's "extraordinary virtuosity with people," his "exquisite consideration," his "politeness that moved so fast and intuitively that it could be examined only in its effect"— all were qualities of Gerald Murphy's, and the Divers' effect on their friends had many echoes in the Murphys' effect on theirs. "People were always their best selves with the Murphys," John Dos Passos, a lifelong friend, said of them. Archibald MacLeish, another old and very close friend, remarked that from the beginning of the Murphys' life in Europe, "person after person—English, French,

American, everybody—met them and came away saying that these people really are masters in the art of living."

Fitzgerald saw this, and something more besides. With his great gift for catching the social tone and texture of his period, Fitzgerald had a tendency to look for the real essence of an era in terms of certain individuals living in it—personal heroes like the "romantic" Princeton football player "Buzz" Law or the maverick Hollywood producer Irving Thalberg. "At certain moments," he wrote in his notes for *The Last Tycoon*, "one man appropriates to himself the total significance of a time and place." For Fitzgerald, Gerald and Sara Murphy embodied the significance of that remarkable decade in France, during which, as he once wrote, "whatever happened seemed to have something to do with art." Even though Fitzgerald himself showed little interest in the art of his time, and ignored it almost completely in *Tender Is the Night*, he did respond to the atmosphere of freshness and discovery that characterized the period.

When the Fitzgeralds arrived in France, in the spring of 1924, the Murphys had been there for three years and had become, according to MacLeish, a "sort of nexus with everything that was going on." In the various apartments and houses they rented in or near Paris, and at a villa they were renovating at Cap d'Antibes, on the Riviera, one met not only American writers like Hemingway and MacLeish and Dos Passos but a good many of the Frenchmen and other Europeans who were forging the art of the twentieth century: Picasso, who had a studio near them in Paris and who came down to visit them in Antibes; Léger, who liked to take them on nocturnal tours of Paris's earthy little cafés, bars, dance halls, and *foires foraines*; Stravinsky, who came to dinner and unfailingly commented on the flavor of the bread, which Sara sprinkled with water and put into the oven before serving. "The Murphys were among the first Americans I ever met," Stravinsky has said, "and they gave me the most agreeable impression of the United States." The couple had come to know most of their European friends through the Ballets Russes of Serge Diaghilev, for whom they had both volunteered to work as unpaid apprentices soon after their arrival in Paris in 1921, when they learned that a fire had destroyed most of the company's scenery. The Murphys, who had been studying painting with one of Diaghilev's designers, Natalia Goncharova, went to the company's atelier in the Belleville quarter to help repaint the décors for *Schéhérazade*, *Pulcinella*, and other ballets, from the original *maquettes*, using long-handled, soft brushes like brooms to apply the color, and climbing up thirty-foot ladders to get the proper perspective. Picasso, Braque, Derain, Bakst, and other Diaghilev artists came by frequently to supervise the work and comment on it. "In addition to being the focal center of the whole modern movement in the arts," Murphy said, "the Diaghilev ballet was a kind of movement in itself. Anybody who was interested in the company became a member automatically. You knew everybody, you knew all the dancers, and everybody asked your opinion on things." The Murphys went to rehearsals, attended the premières, and were invited to the spectacular soirées at the house of the ballet's great patroness, the Princesse de Polignac (née Winifred Singer, heiress to the Singer sewing machine fortune, a formidable American woman, whose profile was said to resemble Dante's and whose ambition, according to Stravinsky, was to have her bust placed next to Richelieu's in the Louvre). They had arrived in Paris at a moment when the twentieth-century revolution in the arts, which had begun before the First World War, was taking a variety of fresh new forms, and when the activity in all fields of art was intense and closely linked. The Cubist juggernaut had been succeeded by the inspired madness of Dada and the aggressive eroticism of the Surrealists. Intellectuals had fallen in love with the popular arts—the movies, the circus, *le jazz hot*. All the arts seemed poised on the verge of a new Golden Age, the product of postwar energies and a sense of personal freedom that encouraged limitless experimentation. "Between 1920 and 1930 nobody doubted but that he was on the way to creating something," the French critic Florent Fels wrote. "We were not out to change the world, but we were trying to make it look different and think differently."

Certainly no two Americans could have been better conditioned than the Murphys were, by background and temperament, to respond to everything that was going on or to feel so thoroughly sympathetic to the excitement of the modern movement. Sara Murphy, the eldest of three daughters of a Cincinnati ink manufacturer named Frank B. Wiborg, had spent a large part of her childhood in Europe with her mother and sisters. The three girls were strikingly beautiful, in entirely different ways: Olga, the youngest, had a serene, classic face; Mary Hoyt ("Hoytie") was dramatic, dark, and intense; and Sara's fresh, delicate beauty and golden hair reflected the family's Scandinavian heritage (their paternal grandfather was Norwegian). The girls had all been given voice lessons, and at parties where, in that era, the guests were often expected to "perform" in one way or another, the Wiborg sisters were a sensation. They had a wide repertory of folk songs, which they sang in three-part harmony (Sara singing contralto, Hoytie tenor, and Olga soprano) with an unselfconscious "American" directness that delighted European listeners. As their *pièce de résistance* they would stand behind a semitransparent curtain, take down the straps of their evening gowns, wave their arms, and sing the Rhine-maidens' theme from *Das Rheingold*. Lady Diana Cooper introduced them to London society. They were presented at the Court of St. James's in 1914, and, as Lady Diana wrote in her autobiography, "That year the Wiborg girls were the rage of London."

By the time she was sixteen Sara Sherman Wiborg (she was named for General William Tecumseh Sherman, her mother's favorite uncle) had learned to speak fluent French, German, and Italian. She was not in the slightest degree impressed by fashionable society, however, and she said just what she thought to everyone. "I love Sara," Lady Diana said to Mrs. Wiborg. "She's a cat who goes her own way." Sara became a great favorite of her mother's friend Stella Campbell (Mrs. Patrick Campbell), who used to insist that Sara accompany her when she went to buy clothes for one of her theatrical roles. "Sara, darling," she would say, in her deep, Italianate voice, "does the dress walk? Or does it make me look just like a cigar?" Gerald Murphy said once that although he had known Sara for eleven years before they were married and could hardly relate an incident in his life in which she did not play a part, she had remained so essentially and naïvely original that "to this day I have no idea what she will do, say, or propose."

Until 1921, Gerald's contact with Europe had been largely vicarious. His father, Patrick Francis Murphy, for twenty-five years spent five months a year studying the details of the upper-class Europeans' way of life and the implements contrived for it, which he screened and, in many cases, improved upon before putting them on sale in the Mark Cross store, then at Fifth Avenue and Twenty-fifth Street. The elder Murphy introduced, among other things, Minton china, English cut crystal, Scottish golf clubs, and Sheffield cutlery, as well as the first thermos bottle ever seen in the United States. Moreover, he designed and marketed the first wrist watch, at the suggestion of a British infantry officer who complained that a pocket watch was too cumbersome for trench warfare.

Patrick Murphy had taken over Mark W. Cross's modest Boston saddlery shop in the eighteen-eighties and built it into an elegant New York store, but he was far from being typical of the successful merchants of the era. He spent most of the day reading the English classics in his office (he had a special passion for Macaulay); he was known as the wittiest after-dinner speaker of his day; and he wrote his own business advertisements—a column in each of the New York newspapers once each week, headed by fifty words of philosophy and wit and ending with a slogan such as "Mark Cross—everything for the Horse but the Rider and Everything for the Rider but the Horse." Furthermore, he had not the slightest desire to become any wealthier than he was. "How many times must I tell you I don't *want* to make more money?" Gerald remembered their father saying when Frederick Murphy, Gerald's older brother, argued for an expansion of the business. Their disputes on this subject led eventually to an estrangement that was not made up until Fred lay dying, as a delayed result of wounds suffered while serving as a tank officer in the First World War. (Along with one other officer in his regiment, Major George S. Patton—who carried a pearl-handled revolver even then—Fred had volunteered for the first French tanks corps, in the days when tank officers ran alongside the tanks to direct their operations.) Fred and Gerald were never particularly close. According to Monte Woolley, the actor, who was a class ahead of Gerald at Yale, "The relation between the brothers was something that always seemed comical to me. Their politeness to one another was formidable. They never relaxed in each other's presence." Gerald's relationship with his sister Esther, who was ten years younger, was also rather ceremonious. A precocious, phenomenally well-read child and a nonstop conversationalist even at age nine, Esther survived two unsuccessful marriages—the second to Chester Arthur, a grandson of the twenty-first President—and later became a permanent resident of Paris.

Gerald Murphy was born in 1888, in Boston. Four years later his father moved the business to New York, and the family re-established itself in a modest brownstone house on lower Fifth Avenue. Although he grew up in comfortable surroundings, Gerald's childhood was not a happy one. His father believed that children should be strictly brought up, and the Murphy children were not allowed to complain; one winter day, when Gerald fell through the ice of the Central Park lake, his father kept him outdoors, his underwear freezing to his skin, until they had completed their walk. Soon after this he was sent away to a Catholic boarding school near Dobbs Ferry, where, he remembered vividly, he was "flogged by nuns" for wetting his bed. The nuns used to take errant boys to an abandoned shed and paddle them with pieces of wood lath. The experience left Gerald with a lifelong antipathy to Catholicism and all its trappings.

Later he went to Hotchkiss, where he graduated in 1907; but because his father thought he was not ready for college, he spent the next year at Andover. Patrick Murphy hoped that his second son would go to Harvard—Fred had already graduated from Yale— but Gerald chose Yale. He soon regretted the decision. "I hated New Haven," he said later, "and never felt I got anything of what I wanted out of it. You always felt you were expected to make good in some form of extracurricular activity, and there was such constant pressure on you that you couldn't make a stand—I couldn't, anyway. The athlete was all-important, and the rest of the student body was trained to watch and cheer from the sidelines. There was a general tacit Philistinism. One's studies were seldom discussed. An interest in the arts was suspect. The men in your class with the most interesting minds were submerged and you never got to know them."

By not making a stand, Murphy was elected to the top fraternity (DKE), was tapped for Skull and Bones, was made manager of the glee club and chairman of the dance committee, and was voted the best-dressed man in the Class of 1912. Tall and handsome, with reddish hair, perfectly assured manners, and a quick intelligence, Gerald was a sort of beau ideal to many of his classmates. Somehow, though, he lacked the competitive drive that

14

would have made his achievements seem worthwhile to him; the qualities that made him a big man in the Class of 1912 did not appear in the least admirable to Murphy. Archibald MacLeish, who was in Bones three years behind Gerald, said that when he and his wife went over to Paris in the twenties, and everybody told them that they must meet the Murphys (he had not known Gerald at Yale), he got the distinct impression that the Murphys were avoiding them; afterward, when they had become close friends, MacLeish decided that Murphy had simply been reluctant to meet another Bones man. The only two college friends that Murphy continued to see much of after his graduation were Monty Woolley and Cole Porter—one of the most interesting minds of the Class of 1913, who owed much of *his* success at Yale to Murphy's friendship.

Murphy loved to describe his first meeting with Cole Porter: "There was this barbaric custom of going around to the rooms of the sophomores, and talking with them to see which ones would be proper material for the fraternities. I remember going around with Gordon Hamilton, the handsomest and most sophisticated boy in our class, and seeing, two nights running, a sign on one sophomore's door saying, 'Back at 10 p.m. Gone to football song practice.' Hamilton was enormously irritated that anyone would have the gall to be out of his room on visiting night, and he decided not to call again on this particular sophomore. But one night as I was passing his room I saw a light and went in. I can still see that room—there was a single electric light bulb in the ceiling, and a piano with a box of caramels on it, and wicker furniture, which was considered a bad sign at Yale in 1911. And sitting at the piano was a little boy from Peru, Indiana, in a checked suit and a salmon tie, with his hair parted in the middle and slicked down, looking just like a Westerner all dressed up for the East. We had a long talk, about music, and composers—we were both crazy about Gilbert and Sullivan—and I found out that he lived on an enormous apple farm and that he had a cousin named Desdemona. He also told me that the song he had submitted for the football song competition had just been accepted. It was called 'Bulldog,' and of course it made him famous."

Famous, but not entirely accepted at Yale. Although he received the second largest personal allowance of any boy in his class (the largest was Leonard Hanna's), Cole Porter did not fit easily into the social mold of a Yale man. At Murphy's insistence, however, he was elected to DKE that year, and soon afterward Murphy persuaded the glee club, of which he was manager, to take Porter in as a sophomore—something that was never done—so that he could sing a new song he had written on the glee club's tour that spring. The song was the hit of the show. It was a satire on the joys of owning an automobile, and Porter came out in front of the curtain to sing it in the next-to-closing spot, with his hands folded behind him, while the seniors and juniors behind him on the stage went "zoom, zoom, zoom."

After graduating from Yale in 1912, Murphy spent the next

five years working for the Mark Cross company. His father expected
both sons to carry on the business—Fred was then running the
Mark Cross factory in England—and Gerald was not as yet
prepared to do anything other than what was expected of him.
The seeds of dissatisfaction had begun to germinate, however; his
Irish imagination rebelled against the life that unrolled so smoothly
in his path. The one person to whom he confided his doubts and
uncertainties was Sara Wiborg.

Gerald and Sara had known each other since 1904.
Soon after the Wiborgs moved from Cincinnati to New York,
Gerald had become a sort of adopted "cousin" to the three Wiborg
girls, looking out for them at parties and dances and visiting them
in the summers at their big house in East Hampton, where Frank B.
Wiborg had bought a six-hundred-acre tract of ocean-front property
bordering on what is now the Maidstone Club. Mrs. Wiborg did
not appear to contemplate the possibility of her daughters' marrying;
she depended on them as companions for her annual travels (one
year they toured India, going by arduous stages as far north as
the Khyber Pass) and as ornaments of her formidable social
existence. By 1914, though, Gerald had begun writing letters to
Sara that were increasingly personal in tone, and among whose
slightly stilted phrases ran a strain of deep melancholy. He admitted
to being subject to frequent "glooms" and depressions: "the black
service do get after me at times," as he put it. He confided to her
his scorn for the social code that prevented a man from discussing

books, music, or paintings with another man, because it would be considered effeminate: "I long for someone with whom, as I walk the links, I can discuss, without conscious effort—and with unembarrassed security—the things that do not smack of the pavement." Of his own life to date, he wrote Sara, "For me it has been a life of such sham and utter unreality (for which I am to blame), that I wish everything that deserves to should go thro' the sieve."

Early in February, 1915, they became engaged. The letters that followed this event—sometimes two or three in a single day—show a man who has suddenly gained confidence in his own instincts, tastes, and desires: "I feel almost as though we alone knew where caskets of gold and jewels were buried. . . . I feel more and more as if we had registered at the office of Civilization a claim to a place in the world—and that it had been granted." Sara's mother strongly opposed the match, without bothering to give reasons, and the weekends at East Hampton became increasingly oppressive. Gerald, who got little support in emotional matters from his own family, occasionally worried that his character would prove too weak "to carry us both over the bumpy parts of life." But an enormous optimism was taking root. The life that he envisioned for them was to be an entirely new experience, something that neither of them had known before and which they would somehow collaborate to bring into being. "Do you know," he wrote her, "I think we shall always enjoy most the things we plan to do of our own accord,—and together, even among others, but in our *own* way." Their life together would be fresh, new, and invented; it would be their own joint imaginative creation.

They were married on December 30, 1915, in New York. For the next two years they lived in a small house at 50 West Eleventh Street, which Patrick Murphy had given them as a wedding present, and which they proceeded to decorate in Victorian style— a rather startling innovation that enabled them to buy inexpensively a number of excellent pieces of furniture that had only recently been discarded as hopelessly "out of date." The first of their three children, Honoria (named for no one in either family), was born two years later. Eleven days after Honoria's birth, Gerald left for Kelly Field, Texas, where he received his basic training in the aviation section of the U.S. Signal Corps. Training for aviation pilots in the First World War consisted then of twelve weeks in ground school, followed by a period of flight instruction somewhere else. After a few more weeks at Roosevelt Field (now Mitchell Field) on Long Island, Murphy was assigned to the Handley-Paige flight training unit in England. The armistice was declared on the day he was due to sail, however, and he returned, somewhat disappointed, to civilian life.

By then Gerald knew that he did not want to continue working for his father at Mark Cross. What, his father inquired, *did* he want to do? Gerald, who had had no clear idea until that moment, announced that he wanted to study landscape architecture.

"I had to say something," he recalled later, "and that's what came out." Bitterly disappointed though he must have been, Patrick Murphy did not try to argue against his son's decision. The young Murphys spent the next two years in Cambridge, where Gerald took the graduate course at the Harvard School of Landscape Architecture. Cambridge seemed to them far more stimulating than New York. They saw quite a lot of Alice James and her circle, and Mrs. Winthrop Chanler introduced them to Amy Lowell. "You must meet her," Gerald wrote to Sara, who had been in New York when he was first introduced. "She knows everything *about* everything—yet she's so cordial and human. I was talking to her alone one time and suddenly she said: 'Repeat that'—I was very much frightened and did. She whipped out a pencil and wrote it down, and said casually: 'Now, go on.' I had merely said that the characters in the Russian novels seemed to me such weak animals that the hopelessness of it all became unreal. She jumped— and kept saying to herself: 'Weak animals, weak animals is right, weak animals is good!' " Gerald also grew fascinated at this time with botany and took courses in it at Harvard. "I feel now that I should like to know all the flowers, trees, grasses, stars, rocks, and the very air itself," he wrote Sara. "It repays one so, the beauty that is revealed *with* the knowledge."

But even in Cambridge the pressure of two powerful and demanding families—Sara's especially—put a strain on the new life that they were trying to create for themselves. There was, in addition, the oppressive sense that conditions in the United States were becoming increasingly unfavorable to innovations of any kind. As Murphy put it, "You had the feeling that the bluenoses were in the saddle over here, and that a government that could pass the Eighteenth Amendment could, and probably would, do a lot of other things to make life in the States as stuffy and bigoted as possible." Early in 1921, like a good many of their fellow countrymen, the Murphys decided to go abroad and live there for a while. Although two more children had come along by this time, there was enough money for all of them to live comfortably in Europe, where the rate of exchange was so highly favorable to Americans; Frank Wiborg had recently divided his fortune into equal shares, and the income from Sara's portion came to seven thousand dollars a year. That spring, with their three children—Honoria, aged three; Baoth, aged two; and Patrick, a baby of eight months—the Murphys sailed for England. They spent a pleasant summer in the countryside; Gerald still planned to become a professional landscape architect, and he wanted to see and study the famous English gardens. In the fall they crossed the Channel and settled for the winter in Paris, first in the Hotel Beau Site and then in an apartment at 2, rue Greuze, near the Étoile.

PARIS

Paris was where the twentieth century was.
—GERTRUDE STEIN

Walking down the Rue de la Boëtie one autumn morning in 1921, soon after their arrival in Paris, Gerald Murphy stopped to look in the window of the Rosenberg gallery, went inside, and saw, for the first time in his life, paintings by Braque, Picasso, and Juan Gris. What he felt at this moment was the shock of discovery: "I was astounded. My reaction to the color and form was immediate. To me there was something in these paintings that was instantly sympathetic and comprehensible. I remember saying to Sara, 'If that's painting, it's what I want to do.'" That day marked the end of Murphy's training as a landscape architect and the beginning of his career as a painter, a career that lasted for nine years, produced, in all, ten remarkable canvases, and ended as abruptly as it began.

His only formal training was with Natalia Goncharova,

the Russian *émigré* artist who also designed sets for the Diaghilev ballet. At the beginning Sara and their friend Hester Pickman (née Chanler) studied along with him, going every morning to Goncharova's studio on the Rue Jacob. Goncharova explained to them the elements of modern painting and made them work exclusively in abstract forms: "She wouldn't let us put on the canvas anything that resembled anything we had ever seen." After six months of this discipline, however, Murphy began to evolve a style of his own, which lay midway between realism and abstraction and which today, forty years later, seems astonishingly close to the ironic factualism of American Pop art. His paintings were often quite large, and they were characterized by hard, flat color and by a meticulous rendering of familiar household objects in the finest detail: a safety razor, the cover of a cigar box, a wasp devouring a pear. He worked very slowly, making many preparatory studies and taking months to complete a picture.

When he exhibited for the first time at the Salon des Indépendants in 1923, however, his boldly composed and technically assured *Razor* caused an immediate stir. Léger announced that Gerald Murphy was the only *American* painter in Paris, meaning the only one who had shown a really American response to the new postwar French painting. Not everyone agreed. Segonzac, one of the judges for the 1924 Indépendants, argued angrily against hanging Murphy's *Boatdeck, Cunarder,* a twelve-by-eighteen-foot canvas showing the stacks and ventilators of the liner *Aquitania;*

he dismissed it as "architectural drawing." He was overruled, and Murphy was photographed for the newspapers standing in front of his gigantic picture, wearing a bowler hat and a cryptic expression. The next year Murphy exhibited a six-foot-square painting of the inside of a watch. Hanging in the same show was a picture by the Spanish artist Joan Miró, then virtually unknown, called *The Farm*, which Ernest Hemingway purchased.

Hemingway and his first wife, Hadley, were living over a sawmill on the Rue Notre Dame des Champs. They had recently gotten to know the Murphys, whom Hemingway thought "grand people," and to whom he had read the entire manuscript of his second novel, *The Torrents of Spring*. Gerald found the book in questionable taste—it was a rather vicious parody of Sherwood Anderson—and Sara, who had been on the point of going to bed when Hemingway arrived unexpectedly at their apartment with his manuscript, slept through most of it, sitting bolt-upright on the sofa. If Hemingway noticed, he gave no sign.

As hundreds of accounts of the era have attested, American expatriate life in Paris in the twenties was, in general, one of rather self-conscious intellectual ferment. For the Murphys, however, it was something different. Older by a decade than most of their fellow expatriates, and leading a relatively stable existence that centered largely on their children, they had little in common with the determined bohemianism of many of the Americans in Montparnasse. Most of their friends were married couples with

children, who, like them, had come to live in Paris primarily
because of a profound discontentment with American life. "Of all
of us over there in the twenties, Gerald and Sara sometimes seemed
to be the only real expatriates," MacLeish once said. "They couldn't
stand the people in their social sphere at home, whom they considered
stuffy and dull. They had enormous contempt for American
schools and colleges and used to say that Honoria must never,
never marry a boy who had gone to Yale. And yet, at the same time,
they both seemed to treasure a sort of Whitmanesque belief in the
pure native spirit of America, in the possibility of an American
art and music and literature."

The Murphys' household, in fact, was a place where their
fellow countrymen could keep up with much that was going on at
home. Gerald had an arrangement with the drummer in Jimmy
Durante's band to send them, in monthly shipments, the latest
jazz records. He imported the new household gadgets being produced
in America (an electric waffle iron, for one), knew the latest
American dances, and read the new American books. The French,
who were fascinated by anything American, used to love to hear the
Murphys sing Negro folk songs and spirituals, which Gerald had
been collecting for years. He had discovered in the Boston Public
Library the texts of many songs sung by Southern Negroes before
the Civil War (songs at that time unpublished anywhere, such
as "Nobody Knows the Trouble I've Seen" and "Sometimes I Feel
like a Motherless Child"), and he and Sara had compiled a

repertory of these, which they sang in two-part harmony, Gerald
singing tenor and Sara alto. They sang them once for Eric Satie.
The eccentric dean of *Les Six* had a lively interest in Americans—he
once wrote that he owed much to Columbus, "because the American
spirit has occasionally tapped me on the shoulder, and I have been
delighted to feel its ironically glacial bite"—and on that occasion
he had come to the Paris house of Mrs. Winthrop Chanler expressly
to hear the Murphys' songs. As they sang, Murphy played a
simple piano accompaniment he had worked out. "After we'd
finished," he recalled, "Mrs. Chanler asked Satie how he liked them,
and he said, 'Wonderful, but there should be no piano. Have them
turn their backs and do it again.' So we did the whole thing over
without accompaniment, and Satie said, 'Never sing them any other
way,' and left."

For the Murphys and their friends, though, America had
not yet caught up with the new century; the center of the world
just then was Paris. In *Paris France*, one of her more lucid books,
Gertrude Stein wrote that between 1900 and 1939 "there really
was a serious effort made by humanity to be civilized. . . . England
had the disadvantage of believing in progress, and progress has
really nothing to do with civilization, but France could be civilized
without having progress on her mind, she could believe in
civilization in and for itself, and so she was the natural background
for this period." Foreigners did not seem romantic to the French;
they were, as Stein said, "just facts." Paris let them alone and at

the same time provided the intellectual nourishment they craved, and, as a result, it was the foreign artists who predominated in the postwar art movements. Diaghilev and Stravinsky, Picasso and Miró, Hemingway and Ezra Pound felt the vibrations and reacted accordingly, and the excitement of their discoveries gave a hectic flush to the atmosphere of the entire period. "Every day was different," Murphy said. "There was a tension and an excitement in the air that was almost physical. Always a new exhibition, or a recital of the new music of *Les Six*, or a Dadaist manifestation, or a costume ball in Montparnasse, or a première of a new play or ballet, or one of Étienne de Beaumont's fantastic 'Soirées de Paris' in Montmartre— and you'd go to each one and find everybody else there, too. There was such a passionate interest in everything that was going on, and it seemed to engender activity."

One of the major events of the spring of 1923, during the Murphys' second year in Paris, was the première of Stravinsky's ballet *Les Noces* by the Diaghilev company. Of all Stravinsky's scores, the one for this powerful work, based on the simple, somewhat savage ritual of a Russian peasant wedding, was Diaghilev's favorite. The impresario was so enthusiastic about it that he had persuaded three well-known composers—Francis Poulenc, Georges Auric, and Vittorio Rieti—to perform three of the four piano parts (Stravinsky had used pianos almost as percussion instruments and had placed them right up on the stage with the dancers); the fourth part was played by Marcelle Meyer, the leading interpreter of the new music and a friend of Sara's and Gerald's. Goncharova executed the décors. The Murphys attended all rehearsals and brought some of their friends, including Dos Passos; he, in turn, brought E. E. Cummings, who sat in the back row and resisted meeting the Murphys. ("I can understand that," Dos Passos explained to them. "I've spent most of my life keeping my friends apart.") Stravinsky relates in his *Memories and Commentaries* that the young Russian choreographer George Balanchine came all the way from Moscow expressly to attend the première.

The excitement over *Les Noces* rose to such a pitch that the Murphys felt moved to celebrate its opening. "We decided to have a party for everyone directly connected to the ballet," he recalled, "as well as for those friends of ours who were following its genesis. Our idea was to find a place worthy of the event. We first approached the manager of the Cirque Médrano, but he felt that our party would not be fitting for such an ancient institution. I remember him saying haughtily, '*Le Cirque Médrano n'est pas encore une colonie américaine.*' Our next thought was the restaurant on a large, transformed *péniche*, or barge, that was tied up in the Seine in front of the Chambre des Députés and was used exclusively by the deputies themselves every day except Sunday. The management there was delighted with our idea and couldn't have been more cooperative." The party was held on June 17, the Sunday following the première. It began at 7 p.m., and the first person to arrive was Stravinsky, who dashed into the *salle à manger* to inspect, and even rearrange, the distribution of place cards. He was apparently satisfied with his own seating—on the right hand of the Princesse de Polignac, who had commissioned *Les Noces*.

Like the famous "Banquet Rousseau," in 1908, at which Picasso and his friends paid homage to Le Douanier Rousseau, the Murphys' *péniche* party has assumed over the years a legendary aura, so that people who may or may not have been there give vivid and conflicting descriptions of the event. The forty-odd people who *were* there constituted a kind of summit meeting of the modern movement in Paris: Picasso; Darius Milhaud; Jean Cocteau; Ernest Ansermet, who had conducted *Les Noces*; Germaine Tailleferre; Marcelle Meyer; Diaghilev; Natalia Goncharova and her husband, Michel Larionov; Tristan Tzara; Blaise Cendrars; and Scofield Thayer, the editor of the *Dial*. There were four or five ballerinas from the company and two of the male principals, but the Murphys had been advised not to invite the whole *corps de ballet*; Diaghilev, a stickler for rank, would not have approved. After cocktails on the canopied upper deck of the *péniche*, the guests drifted downstairs to the *salle à manger*, all except Cocteau, whose horror of seasickness was so excruciating that he refused to come on board until the last Seine excursion boat, with its rolling wake, had gone by.

The champagne dinner that followed was memorable, as was the décor. Having discovered at the last moment that it was impossible to buy fresh flowers on a Sunday, the Murphys had gone

to a bazaar in Montparnasse and bought up bags and bags of toys—
fire engines, cars, animals, dolls, clowns—and they had arranged
these in little pyramids at intervals down the long banquet table.
Picasso was entranced. He immediately collected a quantity of
toys and worked them into a fantastic "accident," topped by a cow
perched on a fireman's ladder. Dinner went on for hours,
interspersed with music—Ansermet and Marcelle Meyer played
the piano at one end of the room—and dancing by the ballerinas.
Cocteau finally came aboard. He found his way into the barge-
captain's cabin and put on the captain's dress uniform, and then
went about carrying a lantern and putting his head in at portholes
to announce gravely, *"On coule"* ("We're sinking"). At one point
Murphy noted with astonishment that Ansermet and Boris
Kochno, Diaghilev's secretary, had managed to take down the
enormous laurel wreath, bearing the inscription *"Les Noces—
Hommages,"* that had been hung from the ceiling, and were holding
it for Stravinsky, who ran the length of the room and leaped
nimbly through the center. No one really got drunk, no one went
home much before dawn, and no one, in all probability, has ever
forgotten the party.

The Murphys left Paris soon afterward to spend the summer
at Antibes. They had discovered the Riviera the preceding summer,
when Cole Porter had invited them down to his rented château
at Cap d'Antibes for two weeks. "Cole always had great originality
about finding new places," Murphy said, "and at that time no

one ever went near the Riviera in summer. The English and the Germans—there were no longer any Russians—who came down for the short spring season closed their villas as soon as it began to get warm. None of them ever went in the water, you see. When we went to visit Cole, it was hot, hot summer, but the air was dry, and it was cool in the evening, and the water was that wonderful jade-and-amethyst color. Right out on the end of the Cap there was a tiny beach—the Garoupe—only about forty yards long and covered with a bed of seaweed that must have been four feet thick. We dug out a corner of the beach and bathed there and sat in the sun, and we decided that this was where we wanted to be. Oddly, Cole never came back. But from the beginning we knew we were going to." There was a small hotel on the Cap that had been operated for thirty-five years by Antoine Sella and his family; ordinarily, it closed down on May 1, when the Sellas went off to manage a hotel in the Italian Alps. In 1923, though, the Murphys persuaded Sella to keep the Hôtel du Cap open on a minimum basis through the summer, with a cook, a waiter, and a chambermaid as the entire staff. They moved in with their children, sharing the place with a Chinese family who had been staying there and had decided to remain when they learned that the hotel would stay open.

The Murphys' regular companions that summer were Picasso and his first wife, Olga; their young son, Paolo; and Picasso's elderly mother, Señora Maria Ruiz. They had come down to visit the Murphys at the Hôtel du Cap and had liked the region so much that they took a villa in nearby Antibes. Olga had been a *deuxième ballerina* in the Diaghilev company. She was a pretty girl with a button mouth and a thin nose, who agreed with everything anyone said, had no conversation, and was entirely prosaic—qualities that Picasso appeared to relish at the time. (Later, when he had left her, she followed him around Paris for three days with a revolver; eventually she went mad.) Señora Ruiz spoke no French at all, only Spanish, but the Murphys got on splendidly with her.

Picasso at that time was working in two radically different styles: the late Cubist phase that produced such milestones as his 1921 *Three Musicians*; and the monumental, figurative style of his classical period, influenced by his recent trip to Rome with Diaghilev. He was struck by the way Sara slung her pearls down her back when she wore them to the beach (it was "good for them to get the sun," she explained), and some of the huge women in his classical paintings and drawings of this period are shown with pearl necklaces thrown over their shoulders in Sara's manner. It was a touch that Scott Fitzgerald later made use of when he described Nicole Diver sitting on the beach, "her brown back hanging from her pearls." Gerald and Sara saw the Picassos nearly every day, and were unfailingly diverted by the painter's sardonic wit. "It was not repartee or badinage on his part," Gerald said, "but a natural counterreaction to things. He never talked about art, and

35

he rarely expressed an idea that was in any way abstract. In fact, the only time I ever remember him saying anything of an abstract sort was one day when we all happened to see an old black farm dog hold up a chauffeur-driven cabriolet by lying stubbornly in the road, in the shade of a fig tree. The chauffeur finally had to get out and shoo him away with a lap robe. Picasso watched the whole pantomime without a shade of expression, and when the car had driven on and the dog had come back to lie down in the middle of the road again, he said, '*Moi, je voudrais être un chien.*' I also remember his habit of creeping up behind people on the beach, waiting for them to stoop over to pick up a shell or something, and then photographing them from the rear. He had a remarkable collection, including some rather well-known people."

Americans seemed to fascinate Picasso. Once, in Paris, he invited the Murphys to his apartment, on the Rue de la Boëtie, for an *apéritif*, and, after showing them through the place, in every room of which were pictures in various stages of completion, he led Gerald rather ceremoniously to an alcove that contained a tall cardboard box. "It was full of illustrations, photographs, engravings, and reproductions clipped from newspapers. All of them dealt with a single person—Abraham Lincoln. 'I've been collecting them since I was a child,' Picasso said. 'I have thousands, thousands!' He held up one of Brady's photographs of Lincoln, and said with great feeling, 'There is the real American elegance!'"

Picasso's reputation then was already immense, but it was

not yet universal. One morning, toward the end of the summer, the Murphys learned that his landlord had demanded that Picasso remove a large oil cartoon that he had drawn on the wall of his garage. The landlord was furious, and Picasso, highly amused, gave him eight hundred francs to have it scrubbed off. Another time, Picasso came down to the beach laughing to himself and brandishing a letter from Gertrude Stein. She had seen, at the Rosenberg gallery in Paris, a painting by him that she very much admired, and she wanted to know whether she could have it in exchange for the portrait that Picasso had done of her and given her (the one that is now in the Metropolitan Museum). The Murphys were shocked, and said so. "Yes," Picasso said, "but I love her so much!" Soon afterward Miss Stein and her friend Alice B. Toklas came down to Cap d'Antibes for a few days. "She and Picasso were phenomenal together," Murphy said. "Each stimulated the other to such an extent that everyone felt recharged witnessing it."

Before the summer was out, the Murphys decided to buy a villa of their own. What they wanted above all was a garden, and they found one on a hill just below the Antibes lighthouse, attached to the home of a French army officer who had spent most of his life as a military attaché in the Near East. The villa itself was a sort of chalet, small and unpretentious, but the garden was extraordinary. Each year, returning on home leave, the owner had brought back exotic trees and plants—date palms, Arabian maples with pure-white leaves, pepper trees, olives, ever-bearing lemon trees, black

and white figs—all of which had prospered and proliferated.
Heliotrope and mimosa ran wild through the garden, which flowed
down from the house in a series of levels, intersected by gravel
paths. There was hardly a flower that would not grow there, for it
was on a side of the hill that was protected from the mistral. At
night, the whole place throbbed with nightingales.

In *Tender Is the Night*, the Divers' villa is actually a cross
between the Murphys' and another house, high up above the
Corniche near Èze, owned by Samuel Barlow, the American
composer. Barlow had razed several ancient peasant cottages to
make his garden and had incorporated several others into his house.
The Murphys went to no such lengths with their property, but
they did undertake a fairly extensive remodeling of the villa, which
required nearly two years to complete. They had the peaked chalet
roof replaced with a sun roof—one of the first sun roofs ever seen
on the Riviera—thus providing a second story and two bedrooms for
the children. They put down an outdoor terrace of gray and white
marble tiles, taking great care to preserve a huge silver linden
tree, under which they later served almost all their meals. With
his unerring eye for good design in everyday objects, Murphy
sought out the dealers who serviced the local restaurants and cafés
and bought a supply of traditional rattan café chairs and plain
deal tables, the legs of which he painted black. Inside, the décor
was a trifle severe (black satin furniture and white walls), but the
house was always full of Sara's flowers from the garden, freshly

picked and arranged every day: oleanders, tulips, roses, mimosa, heliotrope, jasmine, camelias.

While the Villa America, as they had decided to call it, was being renovated, the Murphys returned to Paris for a winter of great activity. Through Léger, who was then executing the sets and costumes for the Milhaud ballet *La Création du Monde*, Murphy had received a commission to create an "American" ballet that would serve as a curtain raiser for the main event. Both were to be put on by the Swedish ballet company then in residence in Paris, the Ballets Suédois. Rolf de Maré, the company's young director, asked Murphy whether he knew of any young American composer in Paris who might do a score in the American idiom, and Murphy, without a moment's hesitation, suggested the matter to Cole Porter. Porter had not yet become a popular success on Broadway, and his wealthy and socially ambitious wife rather hoped that he would devote his talent to "serious" music. The preceding summer, in fact, she had invited Stravinsky down to Antibes to teach her husband harmony and composition; after a consultation with the Murphys, Stravinsky had declined.

Porter readily agreed to write a score for the Swedish ballet company, though, and he and Murphy worked together on this project at the Porters' palazzo in Venice for three weeks during the summer of 1923. The result of their collaboration was *Within the Quota*, a lively thirty-minute work satirizing the impressions of a young Swedish immigrant to the United States. Gerald worked out the story line and painted a striking backdrop, which was a parody of the Hearst newspapers of the day; it included an ocean liner standing on end beside the Woolworth Building and a variety of lurid headlines, and across the top ran a banner reading, "UNKNOWN BANKER BUYS ATLANTIC." ("*C'est beau, ça,*" Picasso remarked to Gerald when the curtain went up on opening night.) Cole Porter's score was a witty parody of the piano music played in silent-movie theaters, with the orchestra attempting now and then to take over but the piano always winning out. Just before the première, Léger had de Maré switch the order of performance; he appeared to feel that the spirited curtain raiser might attract too much attention away from the main work. Both ballets, in any case, were warmly received.

That spring the Murphys rented a house that had belonged to Gounod, and still remained in his family, on a hill in St.-Cloud, overlooking Paris. Archibald MacLeish's poem "Sketch for a Portrait of Mme. G—— M——" describes Sara in terms of her sitting room in this lovely old house ("Its fine proportions in that attitude/Of gratified compliance worn by salons/Whose white-and-gold has settled into home") and expresses, incidentally, what all the Murphys' friends remarked on at one time or another— their talent for making any place they lived in seem a revelation of their own personalities. The Murphys did not entertain lavishly. Although Andrew Turnbull's biography of Scott Fitzgerald has them giving parties for forty people at Maxim's, with Murphy tipping the coatroom attendant in advance to spare "the poorer artists" in his group any embarrassment ("My God!" Murphy exclaimed after reading that. "Can you imagine anything more arrogant?"), the fact was that neither he nor Sara could stand large parties (which Sara called "holocausts"), and, with the exception of the fête for *Les Noces* and one or two others, they never gave them. "It wasn't parties that made it such a gay time," Sara said. "There was such affection between everybody. You loved your friends and wanted to see them every day, and usually you did see them every day. It was like a great fair, and everybody was so young."

Work on the Villa America was proceeding slowly, and when the Murphys went down to Antibes for the summer of 1924, they had to put up again at the Hôtel du Cap. Several of their friends visited them there: Monte Woolley; Gilbert Seldes and his wife (on their honeymoon); the Picassos again; and the Count and Countess Étienne de Beaumont, Proustian characters who were great connoisseurs and patrons of the avant-garde. (One of the literary events of 1924 was the publication of the late Raymond Radiguet's second novel, *Le Bal du comte d'Orgel*, and it was common knowledge that Radiguet's Count d'Orgel had been modeled on Étienne de Beaumont.) Rudolph Valentino stayed at the hotel for a few days, to Honoria Murphy's breathless delight, and bathed from the beach that Gerald was slowly clearing of seaweed at the rate of about eight square feet a day.

Later on, in August, Scott and Zelda Fitzgerald arrived. The Murphys had met the Fitzgeralds in Paris that spring. Scott and Zelda had announced that they were fleeing the hectic social life on Long Island, and in June they settled in St.-Raphaël, where they planned to live on "practically nothing a year." When they came over to visit the Murphys at the Hôtel du Cap, it was evident that the quiet life had so far eluded them. Zelda had fallen in love with a French aviator. Although Scott had found out about it and the affair had been broken off, both of them were on edge. One night, after everyone had gone to bed, the Murphys were awakened by Scott, who stood outside their door with a candle in his violently trembling hand. "Zelda's sick," he said; he added in a tense voice, as they hurried down the hall, "I don't think she did it on purpose." She had swallowed a large, but not fatal, quantity of sleeping pills, and they had to spend the rest of the night walking her up and down to keep her awake. For the Murphys, it was the first of many experiences with the Fitzgeralds' urge toward self-destruction. Later in their stay, when Sara remonstrated with them for their dangerous habit of coming back late from parties and then, on Zelda's initiative, diving into the sea from thirty-five-foot rocks, Zelda turned her wide, penetrating eyes on her and said innocently, "But, Sara"—she pronounced it "Say-ra"—"didn't you know? We don't believe in conservation."

Toward the end of the summer, work on the Villa America had progressed far enough for the Murphys to move in, and from

that time until they left Europe for good, ten years later, it was
their real home. They also kept a small apartment on the Quai des
Grands-Augustins, on the Left Bank, and they went up to Paris at
least once a month and stayed in close touch with everything that
was going on in the capital (that winter, Gerald exhibited his
six-by-six-foot "miniature on a giant scale" of the inside of a watch at
the Salon des Indépendants). But Cap d'Antibes was now their
base. Murphy had converted a gardener's cottage into a studio,
where he worked for several hours each day. Another small farmhouse,
or *bastide*, on the property had been made over into a guest cottage.
The children—then six, five, and three—were overjoyed by the
new arrangements, and it seemed to most of the Murphys' friends
that the life they had set out with such imagination to create for
themselves had fallen into its true pattern and rhythm.

AN ALBUM

Gerald Clery Murphy.

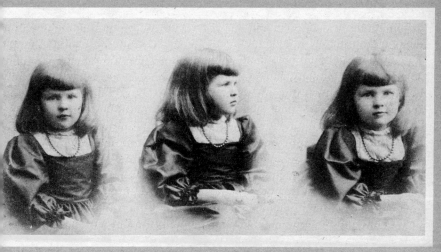

Sara Sherman Wiborg.

Gerald as a young New York merchant—
the role was never a congenial one.

"That year the Wiborg girls were the rage of London." Olga (*left*), Sara Sherman (*center*), and Mary Hoyt Wiborg in 1914.

Gerald in 1917, after completion of
pre-flight training.

Sara's engagement picture. October 17, 1915.

The Murphys were married in December 1915. Honoria, their first child, was born two years later. Baoth arrived in 1919, and Patrick (*next page*) in 1920. "How alike we are," Sara wrote on the back of this 1920 photo (*below*) of herself and Baoth.

The family sailed for Europe in the spring of 1921, with "permanent resident" stamped on their passports. They settled in Paris and spent the summer of 1922 at Houlgate on the Normandy coast. The weather was chilly and wet. They had not yet discovered the summer Riviera.

"Every day was different" in Paris. "Always a new exhibition, or a recital of the new music, or a Dadaist manifestation, or a costume ball in Montparnasse. . . ."

The Murphys' style was elegantly individualistic. Gerald, who hated to carry anything in the pockets of his clothes, sometimes wrapped up personal items in squares of colored cloth. His usual carrying case was a small, expandable leather envelope whose prototype he had seen used by runners of the Paris Bourse to carry banknotes.

Cap d'Antibes, 1923.

A picnic on the Plage de la Garoupe. Among the seated guests in the lower photo are Picasso and his mother, Señora Ruiz (in black), and the Count and Countess Étienne de Beaumont (the Count in a tall white hat, the Countess in a beaded swim suit).

Picasso with his first wife, Olga,
who had been a dancer with the
Diaghilev company.

Sara (*above, with Picasso*) had a way of making each day a festive occasion. "*Sara est très festin,*" Picasso said once, approvingly.

Gerald and Sara with Cole Porter and the Murphys' friend Ginny
Carpenter, in Venice, summer of 1923. Gerald had come to collaborate with
Porter on their ballet, *Within the Quota*.

Gerald, Cole, and the Porters' friend Sir Charles Mendl at the Lido.

Within the Quota, the Porter-Murphy ballet with choreography by Jean Borlin, was presented at the Théâtre des Champs-Élysées in Paris in the fall of 1923. Murphy's costumes (*left*) and his painted backdrop (*above*) satirizing the Hearst newspapers attracted nearly as much comment as Porter's lively score.

The Villa America was finally ready for occupancy in the late summer of 1924. With its sweeping view of sea and mountains (*above*), its lush garden and shaded terrace, it seemed the ideal setting for a life that was "fresh, new, and invented."

Some 1924 visitors—Monty
Woolley, with Baoth (*above*);
Rudolph Valentino at La Garoupe
(*above, right*); Ernest Hemingway
with his son John ("Bumby").

Zelda and Scott Fitzgerald.

Monty Woolley
and Cole Porter.

The Fitzgeralds at Antibes, with their daughter, Scottie.

The Murphy children called their father "Dow-Dow" and delighted in his daily rituals. Sara's deep contentment fascinated Scott Fitzgerald; he once described her face as looking "hard and lovely and pitiful."

Gerald's "functional" sailor's
jersey and white work cap
became standard gear on the
summer Riviera.

Gerald dispensing mid-
morning sherry at La
Garoupe.

The sloop *Honoria,* second of the Murphys' three boats, at its launching in Bordeaux.

Sara and the children, winter of 1925.

Family portraits by Man Ray, summer of 1926.

Salon de Jeunesse. Honoria asked Picasso how to finish her portrait of a horse (*bottom right on screen*). He told her to leave it the way it was. Later that summer the commander of the British Mediterranean Fleet came to lunch at Villa America, and Honoria gave him a painting she had done of his flagship, anchored in the bay. He cabled from shipboard: "*Suis enchanté de tes dessins merci infiniment au revoir jusqu'au prochain* pillow fight *attention aux fisssh* love from The Admiral."

Villa America. Gerald
on the balcony (*left*) and
with Patrick in his studio
(*below*).

In Vienna with Archibald and Ada MacLeish.

The camp near St. Tropez, where the Murphy children found
buried treasure.

On a trip to California in 1932, the family stopped off in
Montana to visit Hemingway.

Montana Vermala, 1929. Baoth, Patrick's nurse,
Sara, Patrick, and Honoria.

Sara's pet monkey, Mistigris.

"Harry's Bar," the Murphys' rented café in Montana Vermala, after renovations.

Venice, 1930.

Bad-Aussee, Austria, 1931. Visits by Léger (*below, right*) and the Fitzgeralds (Scottie Fitzgerald is between Sara and Patrick) made it gayer.

The *Weatherbird*—drawn to scale on the lawn outside Patrick's hospital window, and (*below*) as she looked in 1931.

Gerald and Patrick, 1930.

Family cruise on the *Weatherbird*, 1932.

Sara.

Ellen and Philip Barry.

Gerald
and (*below*) John and Katy Dos Passos.

Fernand Léger and his wife, Jeanne, to whom
the Murphys gave their pet monkey
when they left Europe for good.

Léger came to Saranac in 1935 and sketched this hospital portrait.

Sara in 1934, with
Ellen Barry (left) and
Pauline Hemingway (right).

Sara in 1941.

"I remember saying to him that for me, only the invented part of life was satisfying, only the unrealistic part. Things happened to you—sickness, birth, Zelda in Prangins, Patrick in the sanatorium, Father Wiborg's death—these things were realistic, and you couldn't do anything about them. 'Do you mean you don't accept those things?' Scott asked. I replied that of course I accepted them, but that I didn't feel they were the important things really."

The Murphys' family albums do not go beyond 1933, the year they came back to America.

ANTIBES

Why should I think of the dolphins at Capo di Mele?
Why should I see in my mind the taut sail
And the hill over St.-Tropez and your hand on the tiller?
— ARCHIBALD MACLEISH, from
"American Letter, for Gerald Murphy"

Those closest to the Murphys found it almost impossible to describe the special quality of their life, or the charm it had for their friends. The beauty of their fragrant garden, looking out over the water toward Cannes and the mountains beyond; the records from Gerald's encyclopedic collection (everything from Bach to the latest jazz); the delicious food that always seemed to appear— exquisitely prepared and served—at the precise moment and under the precise circumstances needed to bring out its best qualities (Provençal dishes, for the most part, with vegetables and fruits from the Murphys' garden, though there was often a typically American dish, such as poached eggs on a bed of creamed corn); the passionate attention to every detail of his guests' pleasure that gave Murphy himself such obvious pleasure; Sara's piquant beauty and wit, and the intense joy she took in her life and her friends; the three beautiful children, who seemed, like most children who inhabit a special private world, to be completely at home in adult company—Honoria, who looked like a Renoir and was dressed accordingly; Baoth, robust and athletic; Patrick, disturbingly delicate, and with a mercurial brilliance that made him seem "more Gerald than Gerald"—all of this contributed to an atmosphere that most people felt wonderfully privileged to share. "A party at the Murphys had its own rhythm, and there was never a jarring note," Gilbert Seldes said. "Both of them had a passion for entertaining and for other people."

The central fact in all this was the marriage itself, which often seemed the most entrancing of all the Murphys' creations. "The marriage was unshakable," according to Dos Passos. "They complemented each other, backed each other up in a way that was absolutely remarkable." As with most good marriages, though, the Murphys' was in many respects a matching of opposites. Sara was not interested in clothes and made no effort to appear chic; she was a natural beauty, with her fine, very fair hair that had recently been cut short and bobbed (when Mrs. Patrick Campbell came down to stay in the *bastide* for a few weeks and saw Sara's bobbed head, she turned aside to Gerald and said, in a tragic undertone, "Think, all that tender weight, gone!"). Sara was frank, direct, even brusque at times; she said what she thought, and she didn't flirt. "Sara is incorruptible," Mrs. Winthrop Chanler once remarked in admiration. "I've never heard her say a silly or indifferent thing." And yet, with all her candor, Sara took her life and her friends largely, delighted in them, and was rarely provoked. Like Stella Campbell, she "didn't care much what people did, so long as they didn't do it in the street and frighten the horses."

Gerald's style, one felt, was a more conscious creation. "Sara is in love with life and skeptical of people," Gerald once told Scott Fitzgerald. "I'm the other way. I believe you have to do things to life to make it tolerable." Gerald's Celtic good looks; his beautiful clothes, which would have seemed a trifle too elegant if anyone else had worn them; his perfectionist attention to subtle gradations of feeling—these sometimes acted as barriers to intimacy, so much so that Fitzgerald once accused him of "keeping people away with charm." "Oh, Gerald could be preposterous in those days," one of their friends recalled. "He'd become wildly enthusiastic about something like pacifism and go around asking if you really *wanted* to kill people, and he loved to talk in aphorisms: 'I think the best way to educate children is to keep them confused,' he would say, and then keep on saying it. Also, at times a chill would descend. He was always the most Irish person I ever knew, and when the black mood came over him, he was absolutely unreachable. But then he could be utterly captivating when he wanted to, which was most of the time. You had this feeling that he was doing all kinds of things for your pleasure, and always with the most exquisite taste."

It was, as MacLeish pointed out, taste in the positive sense—

not simply the opposite of bad taste—that the Murphys lived by. "Gerald could take something you hadn't even noticed and make you see how good it was," MacLeish said. "He knew all about Early American folk art, for example, long before the museums started collecting it, and he could tell you the towns along the New England coast where you could go and see marvelous old weather vanes or painted signs. He always had this capacity for enriching your life with things he had found—like those old Negro spirituals or his collection of rare recordings of the early Western songs, which Nicholas Nabokov used when he wrote the music for our *Union Pacific* ballet. Gerald had no interest at all in poetry until I introduced him to Gerard Manley Hopkins, and that set him off; he used to pin a Hopkins poem to his shaving mirror every morning, and he could recite a good many of them. In return, he gave me back Wordsworth, whom I had long abandoned and thought dreadfully dull. Just four lines he'd seen, and how they sprang out!"

In the early twenties Antibes was still a sleepy provincial village. The telephone service shut down for two hours at noon and ceased altogether at seven p.m. The local movie house operated only once a week, and had a piano player who performed with a cigarette dangling from his lip; Léger loved the place, which he said "smelled of feet." There was a new little casino in Juan-les-Pins, where the Murphys and their friends sometimes went in the evenings. The long, quiet days centered on the beach, the garden, and the port, where from 1925 on the Murphys kept a boat. They loved to cruise and had a succession of boats, beginning with a small sloop, the *Picaflor*, progressing through a somewhat larger one, named for Honoria, and culminating in the hundred-foot schooner *Weatherbird*, which was designed and built by a member of the Diaghilev ballet troupe, Vladimir Orloff, who had attached himself to the Murphy family in Paris and had come down to live in Antibes when they built the Villa America. Orloff, the son of a Russian nobleman who managed the private bank account of the Tsarina, had seen his father murdered by the Bolsheviks soon after the October Revolution; escaping from Russia, he had made his way to France, where, like so many of the young White Russian *émigrés*, he gravitated to Diaghilev. He worked for Diaghilev as a set designer, but his real métier, born of a childhood spent on his grandfather's yachts on the Black Sea, was naval architecture. He designed the *Weatherbird* along the lines of the American clipper ships, which he considered the most beautiful vessels ever launched. The *Weatherbird* took its name from a Louis Armstrong record with that title, which the Murphys had sealed in its keel.

Life at the Villa America was too varied to allow for the establishment of any sort of daily routine. The Murphys often had friends staying with them, in the *bastide* or at the Ferme des Orangers, a donkey stable that they had converted into a fully equipped housekeeping cottage in an orange grove across the road from the Villa America. (Robert Benchley, who spent a summer there with

97

his wife and two sons, rechristened it "La Ferme Dérangée".) They
also traveled a good deal, not only to Paris and back but all
around Europe. In the spring of 1926, they went with John Dos
Passos and his wife to visit the Hemingways at Schruns, in the
Austrian Alps. Skiing was just starting to become popular in Europe.
Hemingway had taken it up with his usual gusto and enthusiasm,
and he was favorably impressed by Gerald's rapid mastery of the
stem turn and the Christiania.

That July, the Hemingways visited the Murphys at Antibes,
and from there the four of them went down to Pamplona for the
July fiesta, accompanied by Hadley Hemingway's friend Pauline
Pfeiffer, a *Vogue* editor who would shortly become the second Mrs.
Hemingway. They stayed in the Quintana Hotel, right across the
corridor from the matadors Villalta and Niño de la Palma. Hemingway
was well known from his previous visits to Pamplona, and because
of that, and also because they were the only Americans in town,
they found themselves a constant center of friendly attention. "We
drank the very dry sherry and ate roasted almonds," Murphy
said, "and every time we sat down anywhere we would be surrounded
by Spaniards who shot wine into Ernest's mouth from their
wineskins. One evening a whole crowd of people suddenly began
pointing at Sara and me and shouting, '*Dansa Charles*-ton! *Dansa
Charles*-ton!' Ernest had put them up to it. The Charleston was
all the rage in America then, but it hadn't really spread to Europe

as yet; Sara and I had just learned it that summer, from a traveling dance team that appeared at the casino in Juan-les-Pins—we invited them for lunch, and they taught the steps to the children and to us. And so right there in the middle of the square in Pamplona, with a little brass band playing some sort of imitation jazz and the crowd just going wild, we got up and demonstrated."

Hemingway also obliged Gerald to make an appearance in the bull ring. "When you were with Ernest, and he suggested that you try something, you didn't refuse," Gerald recalled dryly. "He suggested that I test my nerve in the ring with the yearlings. I took along my raincoat and shook it about, and all of a sudden this animal—it was just a yearling and the horns were padded, but it looked about the size of a locomotive to me—came right for me, at top speed. Evidently, I was so terrified that I just stood there holding the coat in front of me. Ernest, who had been watching very carefully to see that I didn't get into trouble, yelled, 'Hold it to the side!' And miraculously, at the last moment, I moved the coat to my left and the bull veered toward it and went by me. Ernest was delighted. He said I'd made a veronica. Ernest himself, meanwhile, was waiting for one of the larger bulls, and a lot of people were watching *him*. Finally he caught the attention of the bull he wanted, and it came toward him. He had absolutely nothing in his hands. Just as the bull reached him, he threw himself over the horns and landed on the animal's back, and stayed there, facing the tail. The bull staggered on a few steps and then collapsed under Ernest's great weight. After that, to my great relief, we went back to our seats."

Although Hemingway adored Sara, he seems to have had reservations about Gerald. He judged men according to his own rigorous standards of masculinity (his favorite comment that summer about someone he admired was "You'd like him—he's tough"), and Gerald, in spite of his performance on skis and in the bull ring, was perhaps not tough enough to suit him. At the same time, Gerald often felt a tacit competitiveness on Hemingway's part. Gerald had always called Honoria "Daughter," and sometimes he would apply the same word to other young women of whom he had grown fond—including Pauline Pfeiffer. He soon noticed that Hemingway had also started calling Pauline "Daughter" and that he didn't like it at all when Gerald did the same. More than once, when Gerald expressed an opinion or an insight with which Hemingway agreed, Hemingway turned on him and said, somewhat resentfully, "You Irish know things you've never earned the right to know." As a result of these undercurrents, Gerald was never as close to Hemingway as he was to Scott and Zelda Fitzgerald.

The Fitzgeralds and the Murphys had seen a great deal of one another in Paris in the winter of 1925–26, during which time Sara and Gerald had assumed, more or less unwittingly, the role of friendly guardians. A decade older than the Fitzgeralds, they looked upon Scott and Zelda's baroque exploits with a mixture of tolerant amusement and genuine concern, and the Fitzgeralds, for their part, often went out of their way to try to shock the Murphys. Scott could not bear to be ignored. If he felt that Sara was not paying enough attention to him, he would do something to upset her. One afternoon in Paris, while riding in a taxi with Sara and Zelda, he pulled out some filthy hundred-franc notes and began putting them in his mouth and chewing them. Sara, whose fear of germs was so intense that she always draped the railway compartments her family traveled in with her own clean sheets, was predictably horrified.

Even in the early days it was an unusual friendship. The two couples had almost nothing in common except their great affection for each other. Neither Scott nor Zelda seemed to have the slightest interest in the art, the music, the ballet, or even the literature of the period; Scott knew the American writers in Paris, and spent a large part of his time that winter getting Hemingway recognized, but he met few Europeans, and he never learned to speak more than a few words of French, which he made not the slightest effort to pronounce correctly. The simpler aspects of the Murphys' life at Antibes—their cultivation of the life of the senses—never appealed to Fitzgerald at all. He scarcely noticed what he was eating or drinking. He stayed out of the sun as much as possible, and his skin never lost its dead-white pallor. When the others on the beach went in swimming, Scott would get up, take a flat running dive into the shallow water, and come right out again. He never

showed any curiosity about Murphy's painting, which he appeared
to consider a mere diversion. Gerald, for his part, was not particularly
impressed with Fitzgerald as a writer. He had not cared much for
The Great Gatsby (Sara had), and neither of them read the
Fitzgerald stories that were appearing—infrequently, just then—in
the *Saturday Evening Post*. "The one we took seriously was
Ernest, not Scott," Murphy said. "I suppose it was because Ernest's
work seemed contemporary and new, and Scott's didn't."

　　None of this seems to have interfered with their spontaneous
liking for each other, however. "We four communicate by our
presence rather than by other means," Murphy wrote to the
Fitzgeralds in 1925. "Currents race between us regardless: Scott
will uncover for me values in Sara, just as Sara has known them in
Zelda through her affection for Scott." Looking back on their
friendship in later years, both Murphys stressed their feeling for
Zelda, whose strange, willful beauty somehow eluded all the
photographs that were taken of her. "Her beauty was all in her
eyes," Gerald said of her. "She had a way of looking directly at
you, an unflinching gaze like an Indian's. And then she moved so
beautifully, with her rangy figure, and she had a great sense of her
own appearance and what was right for her—dresses that were full
and graceful, and bright colors. Her favorite flower was the peony.
They grew in our garden, and Zelda would often pull a bunch
and pin them to her dress, and they suited her somehow."

　　Like Sara, Zelda had her own personal style that owed very

odd things. One day she and Sara were sitting at a table in the
casino at Juan-les-Pins, just the two of them, when a man Sara
knew came over to be introduced. Zelda smiled her lovely smile and
sweetly murmured a taunt of her Alabama school days—"I hope
you die in the marble ring"—but not quite loud enough to be
heard by the man, who thought she was making the usual pleasantry.
Another time, late in the evening, Zelda got up from the table at
the casino where she had been sitting with Scott and the Murphys
and began to dance all by herself on the floor, her skirt raised
above her waist. Startled at first, the Murphys and the others
present soon realized that she was dancing for no one but herself,
as innocently absorbed as a child. "The strange thing was that no
matter what she did—even the wildest, most terrifying things—she
always managed to maintain her dignity," Sara said. "She was a
good woman, and I've never thought she was bad for Scott, as
other people said." The Murphys' feeling for Zelda sometimes
bothered Scott, who would demand to know whether they "liked
Zelda better than me."

The summer of 1926, which began so gaily, ended by putting
a severe strain on the Fitzgerald-Murphy relationship. The
Fitzgeralds had taken a villa in Juan-les-Pins, and their daily yen for
excitement—their restless urge to make something happen wherever
they were—found more outlets than it had the previous summer.
The Riviera was no longer the quiet summer retreat it had been

in 1923. It had begun to fill up with Americans, for one thing. Some were or became friends of the Murphys: the Charles Bracketts and their two children; Alexander Woollcott; the MacLeishes; the Philip Barrys (Barry would later use the Murphys' terrace as the setting for his play *Hotel Universe*). But a good many more were not. The Hôtel du Cap was filled to capacity, and the little Garoupe beach now had a row of bathhouses for its clientele.

The Murphys' life still revolved around their children and their beautiful garden, and they did not participate in the sort of high jinks that the Fitzgeralds were forever cooking up, such as kidnapping waiters and threatening to saw them in half. Even so, the Murphys, with their children and their house guests, their amusing talk, and their mid-morning ritual of dry sherry and sweet biscuits, were generally the focus of the day's activities on the beach that Gerald had reclaimed. Far from snubbing newcomers, Gerald usually contrived, as Fitzgerald later wrote of Dick Diver, to make all encounters "yield the utmost from the materials at hand." Gerald and Monte Woolley took a liking that summer to Sir Charles Mendl, a gentleman whose speech was so impenetrably British that it was often difficult to understand a word he said. One morning they asked him to explain just what the British meant when they called someone a "cad." After considerable thought Sir Charles blurted out, "Oh, hang it, a cad is just someone who makes you go all crinkly-toes!" Mendl later turned up in *Tender Is the Night* as the homosexual Campion, an unflattering and highly inaccurate portrait.

The Murphys seemed by and large to set the style of the place, even down to such details as the clothes people wore. Gerald, who was always interested in "functional" attire, had taken to wearing the traditional French sailors' striped jersey and white work cap, which he bought in a seamen's supply store; with white duck pants, this became a kind of uniform on the Cap d'Antibes that summer. Gerald and Sara sought out the little country restaurants and cafés in the mountains, and because they liked to share their discoveries with their friends, others learned of these places and went there. Fitzgerald's attitude toward the Murphys' style of living, and especially toward Gerald, had by this time become somewhat ambivalent. His affection for Sara was close to an infatuation. He would sit gazing at her across the dinner table for long periods, and if she failed to notice he would say, "Sara, look at me." Sara made light of these attentions. "Scott was in love with all women," she said once. "He'd try to kiss you in taxis and things like that, but what's a little kiss between friends?" Zelda, whose jealousies were notable, was never jealous of Sara. For Gerald, Scott sometimes evinced an absolute and uncritical admiration. Feeling that the older man's superb taste must apply to everything, he would even ask Gerald for advice on literary matters. At the same time, Fitzgerald often seemed to be under a compulsion to ridicule Murphy's elegant style. "I suppose you have some special plan for us today," he would jeer, upon meeting Murphy at the beach. Once, on the terrace at the Villa America, Murphy held up a hand and said mock-portentously, "I hear a pulsing motor at the door." "God, how that sort of remark dates you," snapped Fitzgerald. Although he was intelligent enough to see that Murphy was not a fop, Fitzgerald could never quite fathom the elegant dandyism of Murphy's clothes, his talk, or his manner; and what he failed to understand sometimes galled him.

Fitzgerald's ambivalence toward the Murphys was probably related to his feeling that they were wealthier than in fact they were. The complex of illusions and emotions in which Fitzgerald always enveloped the rich is well known, and once, in a letter to Edmund Wilson, he coupled the Murphys with Tommy Hitchcock as his only "rich friends"; he seems to have had no understanding of the gulf that lay between the Hitchcocks' scale of living and the Murphys'. He often asked Murphy, in his naïve way, what their annual income was, and when Murphy would try to explain that they did not live entirely on income—that they simply spent what they wanted to spend and constantly reduced their capital to do so— Fitzgerald would merely look blank. Scott and Zelda lived poorly on a great deal of money; the Murphys lived extremely well on considerably less. They had no rich friends and took pains to avoid the sort of wealthy society people who had started coming down to Cannes and Nice in the summer. Their distaste for what

Gerald called "*sheer* society" had led, in fact, to a complete break between Sara and her unmarried sister Hoytie (Mary Hoyt Wiborg), whose titled English friends the Murphys refused to invite to their house.

But the Murphys' money was inherited, and they had more of it than most of the people around them; and since they *did* live extremely well, Fitzgerald's affection for them was tainted with some of the animosity and awe that he inevitably felt for the very rich. When he was drinking heavily, as he did more and more that summer, this hostility took concrete form. He was scornful of the idea of a caviar-and-champagne party the Murphys gave one evening at the casino in Juan-les-Pins, and he set out quite deliberately to wreck it. "He made all sorts of derogatory remarks about the caviar-and-champagne notion to begin with, evidently because he thought it the height of affectation," Murphy recalled. "We were all sitting at a big table on the terrace—the MacLeishes and the Hemingways and a few others—and when a beautiful young girl with a much older man sat down at the next table, Scott turned his chair all the way around to stare at them, and stayed that way until the girl became so irritated that the headwaiter was summoned. They moved to another table. Then Scott took to lobbing ashtrays over to a table on the other side of us. He would toss one and double up with laughter; he really had the most appalling sense of humor, sophomoric and—well, trashy. The headwaiter was summoned again. It was getting so unpleasant that I couldn't take it any more, so I got up and left the party. And Scott was furious with me for doing so."

Not long afterward, the Murphys gave a party at the Villa America that could have been, and probably was, the model for the Divers' famous dinner party in *Tender Is the Night*. Fitzgerald again seemed to be under some compulsion to spoil the evening that he later recreated with such sensitivity in his novel. He started things off inauspiciously by walking up to one of the guests, a young writer, and asking him in a loud, jocular tone whether he was a homosexual. The man quietly said, "Yes," and Fitzgerald retreated in temporary embarrassment. When dessert came, Fitzgerald picked a fig from a bowl of pineapple sherbet and threw it at the Princesse de Caraman-Chimay, a house guest of the Murphys' friend and neighbor, the Princesse de Poix. It hit her between the shoulder blades; she stiffened for a moment and then went on talking as if nothing had happened. At this point, MacLeish took Fitzgerald aside, suggested that he behave himself, and received for his pains, without warning, a roundhouse right to the jaw. Then Fitzgerald, apparently still feeling that not enough attention was being paid him, began throwing Sara's gold-flecked Venetian wineglasses over the garden wall. He had smashed three of them this way before Gerald stopped him. As the party was breaking up, Gerald went up to Scott (among the last to leave) and told him that he would not be welcome in their house for three weeks, a term of banishment that was observed to the day.

Such incidents were bad enough, but the Murphys were even more disturbed by the Fitzgeralds' accelerating process of self-destruction. Scott's work was practically at a standstill. Although he talked about the new novel he was writing (the book that became, after eight years and countless revisions, *Tender Is the Night*), he hardly ever seemed to be working. Fitzgerald produced no short stories at all from February, 1926, until June, 1927. He was often depressed and uneasy about his talent, and his drinking was an increasingly serious problem.

Most of the Fitzgeralds' spectacular escapades that summer, which have been enshrined in the Fitzgerald canon by his biographers, were blatantly self-destructive: Zelda plunging down a flight of stone steps because Scott had gone to pay obeisance to Isadora Duncan at the next table; Scott and Zelda returning from dinner with the Murphys at a restaurant in Saint-Paul-de-Vence, driving their little car onto a trolley-car trestle, and falling sound asleep there until early the next morning, when a farmer saw them and pulled their car to safety a few minutes before the trolley was due; Zelda throwing herself under the wheels of their car after a party and urging Scott to drive over her, and Scott starting to do so. Their behavior alienated a good many people that summer, but the Murphys stuck by them and worried deeply about them both. "What we loved about Scott," Gerald said, "was the region in him where his gift came from, and which was never completely buried. There were moments when he wasn't harassed or trying to shock you, moments when he'd be gentle and quiet, and he'd tell you his real thoughts about people, and lose himself in defining what he felt about them. Those were the moments when you saw the beauty of his mind and nature, and they compelled you to love and value him."

The Fitzgeralds went home to America in December, and the Murphys had what Sara, in a letter to Scott and Zelda, described as a "grand quiet spring" following "a dash through Central Europe with the MacLeishes." "But we never got to Russia as planned," she added, "as by the time we got the visas the theaters had closed and the snow started to melt, not to mention the opening of the season for executions." The summer of 1927 was relatively quiet, too, without the Fitzgeralds to contend with. Murphy painted steadily all summer. Léger came down to stay in the *bastide*, unencumbered by his wife. "Fernand's wife, Jeanne, was a man-eater," Gerald said. "We always liked her, but she had a teasing, mocking quality that he found unbearable. She could be terribly funny. He brought her once to a soirée at the Princesse de Polignac's in Paris, a very grand affair with all the big names present. As usual in such a situation, Léger was stiff and taciturn. When it came time to hear the music for the new ballet that the Princesse had commissioned—it was Stravinsky's *Oedipe Roi*— Jeanne Léger, who was sitting next to us in a white dress, with her arms bare to the shoulder, suddenly began to scratch her arms violently and called across to us in a loud stage whisper, 'There are fleas at the Princesse de Polignac's, just like everywhere else!' Poor Fernand was mortified."

The Fitzgeralds had settled outside Wilmington after a brief, riotous sojourn in Hollywood, and the news from and about them was far from reassuring. But when they decided to come over to Europe for the summer of 1928, the Murphys were delighted. "It will be great to see you both again, because we are very fond of you both," Murphy wrote. "The fact that we don't get on always has nothing to do with it."

Nobody got on with Scott and Zelda that summer. Scott's drinking was worse than ever. Zelda's sudden decision, at the age of twenty-eight, to become a professional ballet dancer led to constant friction between them, although Scott outwardly supported her efforts and got Murphy to arrange for her to take lessons with Madame Lubov Egarova, the head of the ballet school for the Diaghilev troupe. For the Murphy chidren, though, the summer was a lovely one. Its highlight was an overnight trip on the sloop *Honoria* to a cove beyond St.-Tropez, where Vladimir Orloff, digging in the sand to pitch a tent, "discovered" an ancient map with detailed instructions, in archaic French, that led them to a series of further clues, and finally, with almost unbearably mounting excitement, to the unearthing of a chest containing key-winder watches, compasses, spyglasses, and (for Honoria) a quantity of glittering antique and imitation jewels. Honoria has said that it was not until years later that any of the children suspected the authenticity of the find.

On a visit to the United States in the late fall of 1928, the Murphy family went across the country by train, stopping off at a ranch in Montana to join the Hemingways and then going on to Hollywood, where Murphy served as consultant to King Vidor on the filming of the all-Negro picture *Hallelujah*. Fitzgerald had told Vidor about Murphy's collection of old Negro songs and spirituals, and Vidor wanted to use them in the film. It was not a completely successful venture; Hollywood was then in the midst of the transition from silent pictures to talkies—*Hallelujah* itself changed to sound in mid-production—and the confusion was total. What saved the day for the Murphys was seeing Dorothy Parker and Robert Benchley, who filled them in on the Hearst-Davies set and the grotesque social life out there.

The following summer, back at the Villa America, was one of the happiest the Murphys had spent, full of gaiety and good friends. The Benchleys came down to visit with their two boys, and so did Dorothy Parker, Donald Ogden Stewart, Ellen and Philip Barry, and several others. Honoria Murphy, then twelve, remembers looking down at the terrace from her bedroom window, seeing the flowers and the lovely food and the ladies in their beaded dresses, and thinking "how it all blended in, and how you just wanted it to last forever." The Fitzgeralds were back again, too, like ghosts at the banquet. Torn and hounded by their personal furies, they would have been difficult company under any circumstances.

But now another strain had been put on their relationship with the Murphys. Scott had decided to use Sara and Gerald as the central characters in his novel, and he was "studying" them openly. His methods were anything but subtle. "He questioned us constantly in a really intrusive and irritating way," Murphy said. "He kept asking things like what our income really was, and how I had got into Skull and Bones, and whether Sara and I had lived together before we were married. I just couldn't take seriously the idea that he was going to write about us—somehow I couldn't believe that anything would come of questions like that. But I certainly recall his peering at me with a sort of thin-lipped, supercilious scrutiny, as though he were trying to decide what made me tick. His questions irritated Sara a good deal. Usually, she would give him some ridiculous answer just to shut him up, but eventually the whole business became intolerable. In the middle of a dinner party one night, Sara had all she could take. 'Scott,' she said, 'you think if you just ask enough questions you'll get to know what people are like, but you won't. You don't really know anything at all about people.' Scott practically turned green. He got up from the table and pointed his finger at her and said that nobody had ever dared say *that* to him, whereupon Sara asked if he would like her to repeat it, and she did."

Sara had felt for a long time that Scott was too wrapped up

in himself to understand even those closest to him, and she was not alone in this opinion. Hemingway warned him in a letter that he had stopped listening to other people, with the result that he heard only the answers to his own questions. Sara put her own irritation succinctly in a note to Scott soon after the incident at the dinner table:

> You can't expect anyone to like or stand a continual feeling of analysis, & subanalysis & criticism—on the whole unfriendly—such as we have felt for quite a while. It is definitely in the air—& quite unpleasant. . . . If you don't know what people are like it's *your* loss. . . . But *you ought to know at your age* that you *can't have Theories about friends*. If you can't take friends largely, & without suspicion—then they are not friends at all.

A subsequent note from Sara was even more explicit:

> We have no doubt of the loyalty of your affections (and we *hope* you haven't of ours) but consideration for other people's feelings, opinions, or even time is *completely* left out of your makeup. . . . You don't even know what Zelda or Scottie [the Fitzgerald's daughter] are like—in spite of your love for them. It seemed to us the other night (Gerald too) that all you thought and felt about them was in terms of *yourself*. . . . I feel obliged in honesty of a friend to write you: that the ability to know what another person feels in a given situation will make—or ruin—lives. . . .
>
> Your infuriating but devoted and rather wise old friend,
>
> Sara

Fitzgerald never replied, but some years later, in a long letter only slightly marred by his usually erratic spelling, he tried to tell Sara a little of what her friendship meant to him:

Dearest Sara

Today a letter from Gerald, a week old, telling me this and that about the aweful organ music around us, made me think of you, and I mean *think* of you (of all people in the world you know the distinction). In my theory, utterly apposite to Ernest's, about fiction i.e. that it takes half a dozen people to make a synthesis strong enough to create a fiction character—in that theory, or rather in despite of it, I used you again and again in *Tender*:

"Her face was hard & lovely & pitiful"
and again
"He had been heavy, belly-frightened with love of her for years"

—in those and in a hundred other places I tried to evoke not *you* but the effect that you produce on men—the echoes and reverberations—a poor return for what you have given by your living presence, but nevertheless an artist's (what a word!) sincere attempt to preserve a true fragment rather than a "portrait" by Mr. Sargent. And someday in spite of all the affectionate scepticism you felt toward the brash young man you met on the Rivierra eleven years ago, you'll let me have my little corner of you where I know you better than anybody—yes, even better than Gerald. And if it should perhaps be your left ear (you hate anyone to examine any single part of your person, no matter how appreciatively

—that's why you wore bright clothes) on June evenings on Thursday from 11:00 to 11:15 here's what I'd say.

That not one thing you've done is for nothing. If you lost everything you brought into the world—if your works were burnt in the public square the law of compensation would still act (I am too moved by what I am saying to write it as well as I'd like). You are part of our times, part of the history of our race. The people whose lives you've touched directly or indirectly have reacted to the corporate bundle of atoms that's you in a *good* way. *I have seen you again & again at a time of confusion take the hard course almost blindly because long after your powers of ratiocination were exhausted you clung to the idea of dauntless courage. . . .*

I know that you and Gerald are one & it is hard to separate one of you from the other, in such a matter for example as the love & encouragement you chose to give to people who were full of life rather than to others, equally interesting and less exigent who were frozen into rigid names. I don't praise you for *this*—it was the little more, the little immeasurable portion of a millimeter, the thing at the absolute top that makes the difference between a World's Champion and an also-ran, the little glance when you were sitting with Archie on the sofa that you threw at me and said:

"And—Scott!"

taking me in too, and with a heart so milked of compassion by your dearest ones that no person in the world but you would have had that little more to spare. . . .

HOME

> *. . . the love of life is essentially as incommunicable as grief.*
> — SCOTT FITZGERALD, letter to
> Sara Murphy, March 30, 1936

ara's warning to Scott was prophetic, although she did not suspect at the time how very close to ruin the Fitzgeralds' lives had veered. Scott and Zelda left Antibes in October to spend the winter in Paris, where Zelda sank deeper and deeper into the schizophrenia that culminated, the following April, in her first mental breakdown. Whether or not Scott fully understood Zelda's illness, he saw pretty clearly what was happening to him, and, with his writer's honesty, he faced up to it squarely in his portrait of Dick Diver. Dick's long "process of deterioration" has its origins, like Fitzgerald's, in a fatal weakness of character; wanting to be good, to be kind, to be brave and wise, Diver "had wanted, even more than that, to be loved." Fitzgerald's own deterioration was traceable in some degree to this same, characteristically American, flaw; the fact that Fitzgerald recognized his self-indulgence and yet never quite gave up the struggle to be an artist gives his life a sort of tragic dignity.

It would be hard to believe that Fitzgerald ever considered Gerald Murphy to be self-indulgent in this sense, or that he attributed the catastrophe that overtook the Murphys in 1929 to anything but a gratuitous slap of fate. Perhaps the strange irony of circumstances helped convince him that he and Zelda and Gerald and Sara were somehow identified—were indeed "the same people"— but there was nothing in the events themselves to justify this notion. In October, 1929, soon after the Fitzgeralds left for Paris, the Murphys' youngest child, Patrick, then nine, developed a persistent fever, which was first diagnosed as bronchitis and then found to be tuberculosis. While Sara and the others remained behind to close the house, Gerald took Patrick to a sanatorium at Montana-Vermala, in the Swiss Alps. This village was the family's home for the next eighteen months.

The Murphys did everything they could to keep their own and Patrick's spirits up during the long ordeal. They rented a chalet on a mountain near the hospital and furnished it with all their customary flair. Friends came to visit—Hemingway, Dos Passos, Dorothy Parker (for six months), Donald Ogden Stewart and his wife—and Fitzgerald came up frequently from Prangins, near Geneva, where Zelda had been placed in a psychiatric clinic. Determined not to succumb to the gloomy atmosphere in the village, nearly all of whose inhabitants were tuberculosis sufferers in one stage or another, Gerald and Sara bought an abandoned little bar and dance hall there, did it over completely in American style, and engaged a five-piece band from Munich to come up and play dance music on Friday and Saturday nights. The family studied charts and planned future Mediterranean cruises on *Weatherbird*, which Vladimir Orloff was then building for them, and whose outlines Gerald one day drew to scale in white lime on the lawn outside Patrick's hospital window. The Murphys' refusal to go under was profoundly moving to their friends. "The memory of a night with the gay Murphys of Paris and Antibes in that rarefied cold silence and atmosphere of death is one of the most terrifying of my life," Stewart once wrote. "But I am prouder of them for that fight for Patrick than for anything else in their lives. The point is, they were not only the most alive, the most charming, the most understanding people—they were, when the roof of their dream house crashed into their beautiful living room, the bravest."

The two older children were away at school through much of this period—Honoria in Paris and Baoth in Munich. They were reunited for the summer in 1931, when Patrick was allowed to leave the sanatorium for a few days at a time. The Murphys had rented an old farmhouse at Bad Aussée in the Austrian Tyrol that summer, and Gerald saw to it that all five of them were photographed in lederhosen and dirndls. Fitzgerald brought Zelda over from Prangins for a "test visit"—her first trip outside the clinic in more than a year. Zelda always felt that the Murphys liked and approved of her in her own right, as an individual rather than as Scott's wife, and she responded well to her stay with them. One evening while she was there, little Scottie Fitzgerald, who was not quite ten, came crying to her mother with the news that she had been forced to bathe in a tub that still contained the water used by Patrick. Sara called the maid, who explained that the bath salts she had put in the water had made it cloudy and led to Scottie's mistake. The incident, which was resolved without hard feelings, later turned up, like so many other incidents that involved the Murphys, in *Tender Is the Night*.

Fitzgerald and Murphy had a long conversation that fall about the strange, sad turnings both their lives had taken. They were riding down on the train together from Montana-Vermala to Munich, to take Baoth out of his school there because Gerald had just learned that he was being made to do military drill outdoors in his underwear and to shout *"Heil Hitler!"* with the others. "Scott had sensed that it would be a difficult errand," Gerald said, "and had asked to come with me. It was one of those times when the best side of him was very evident—he was gentle, and warm, and he listened. Why was it, he asked, that Sara and I always seemed to do things differently from other people? We dressed differently, we lived differently, our parties were different, and so on. I remember saying to him then that for me, only the invented part of life was satisfying, only the unrealistic part. Things happened to you—

sickness, birth, Zelda in Prangins, Patrick in the sanatorium, Father Wiborg's death—these things were realistic, and you couldn't do anything about them. 'Do you mean you don't accept those things?' Scott asked. I replied that of course I accepted them, but that I didn't feel they were the important things really. It's not what we do but what we do with our mind that counts, and for me only the *invented* parts of our life had any real meaning." His words seemed to strike a chord in Fitzgerald, who once wrote that he used to think life was something you dominated if you were any good. In any case, Murphy said, one must learn not to take life at its *own* tragic valuation.

After a year and a half in Switzerland, Patrick was thought to be cured, and the Murphys returned to Antibes and the Villa America. They would spend two more years there, years that were in a sense a coda to the decade that had ended so jarringly for so many people in 1929. Many of their friends had gone home to America. Murphy no longer painted; he had stopped abruptly when Patrick first became ill, and he never took it up again. (The Galerie Bernheim Jeune in Paris gave a one-man show of his pictures in 1936; of the nine paintings in that exhibition, four are now lost and presumably destroyed.) The Murphys spent a great part of their time cruising on their new schooner, the *Weatherbird*. But the world was changing, and the Riviera had lost its innocence. Putting into a tiny Italian harbor one day, they were surrounded by a group of swimmers shouting, *"Mare nostrum!"* And when they went ashore they found pictures of Mussolini plastered on every wall. At Antibes, the Hôtel du Cap was now the Grand Hôtel du Cap, and its expensive new Eden-Roc swimming club functioned from mid-June to mid-August as an adjunct of the American film colony. "At the most gorgeous paradise for swimmers on the Mediterranean," Fitzgerald wrote, "no one swam any more, save for a short hangover dip at noon. . . . The Americans were content to discuss each other in the bar." Then in 1933, Patrick's symptoms suddenly recurred in a new and grave form, and the Murphys decided it was time to go home. They sold the *Weatherbird* (to a Swiss, who was arrested after the war for using it to smuggle gold from Turkey into France), closed the Villa America against their eventual return, and sailed for New York. They never went back.

By the time *Tender Is the Night* came out, in 1934, the era, the places, and the emotions that the book evoked seemed fairly remote to the Murphys. Dick Diver did not seem to have much to do with Gerald, and if Fitzgerald had drawn a great many details, conversations, and incidents from life, he had somehow managed to leave out most of the elements of the Murphys' experience in Europe that mattered most to them: the excitement of the modern movement in Paris, the good friends, the sensuous joy of living at Cap d'Antibes. And yet, in a letter written from the depths of his grief in August, 1935, Gerald told Scott, "I know now that what you said in *Tender Is the Night* is true. Only the invented part of our life—the unreal part—has had any scheme, any beauty. Life itself has stepped in now and blundered, scarred and destroyed." Baoth, the Murphys' older son, a strapping and indefatigable boy who had scarcely been sick a day in his life, had caught measles that spring at the boarding school he was attending, and without warning it had developed into spinal meningitis; he died almost immediately, before Sara and Gerald could get there. "In my heart I dreaded the moment when our youth and invention would be attacked in our only vulnerable spot, the children," Gerald wrote to Scott. "How ugly and blasting it can be, and how idly ruthless." A year and a half later, in January, 1937, the long fight to save Patrick's young life ended in a hospital in Saranac Lake.

One of the things that kept Murphy going during these years was the necessity of coping with a family economic crisis. The Mark Cross company, from which he had escaped so happily years before, had gone precipitously downhill since the death of Patrick Francis Murphy, in 1931, and it was now about a million dollars in debt and under pressure to declare itself bankrupt. Murphy was obliged to assume responsibility for the firm. Taking over the management, he retained full control for the next twenty-two years, during which time he cleared the debts, moved the store to its present Fifth Avenue address, and applied his imagination and taste to a variety of new items, which proved reasonably profitable. But the work, he said, was never congenial and often seemed like sleepwalking. "There is something about being struck *twice* by lightning in the same place," he once wrote to a friend. "The ship foundered, was refloated, set sail again, but not on the same course, nor for the same port."

There is a mordant Spanish proverb that Gerald Murphy once discovered: "Living well is the best revenge." In the years after they left Europe, the Murphys continued to live as well as their somewhat reduced circumstances allowed, first in Manhattan and then in a pre-Revolutionary stone house, which they restored, in the small Rockland County community of Snedens Landing, overlooking the Hudson River. They kept in touch with their old friends—the Dos Passoses, the MacLeishes, Dorothy Parker, Cole Porter. When a mutual acquaintance delivered their affectionate regards to Picasso in 1962, Picasso replied, "Tell Sara and Gerald that I am well, but that I'm a millionaire and I'm all alone." In later years they drew considerable solace from the family that Honoria and her husband, William Donnelly, were raising in Washington, D.C.: two grandsons, John and Sherman; and a granddaughter, Laura.

Gerald followed closely the new movements in art, music, and literature. Curiously, having never particularly cared to own paintings, they never bought any of the work of the modern masters who were their friends. In their summer cottage at East Hampton, though, there was one magnificent Léger, which they acquired by what Murphy considered a small miracle. Léger made his first trip to the United States in 1931 as the Murphys' guest (he was seasick the whole way across). The Murphys saw to it that he met

all the right people, and they commissioned him to do two
paintings, which they donated immediately to the Museum of
Modern Art. Three years later, at the vernissage of a large Léger
retrospective exhibition at this museum, the artist came up to Gerald
and Sara and said that there was one picture in the show he
wanted them to have and that he would present it to them as a gift
if they could pick it out. There were more than two hundred
canvases on view, and Gerald quickly despaired of fixing on the right
one. But as he and Sara descended a flight of stairs she pointed to
a picture on the wall at the foot of the stairway and said, "I think
I see it." The colors, mostly muted browns and reds, were unlike
anything they had ever known him to use before. While they
were looking at it, Léger came up behind them and said, "I see
you've found it." He turned the painting around and showed them,
written on the frame, "*Pour Sara et Gérald.*"

Whatever their feelings toward *Tender Is the Night*, the
Murphys never wavered in their loyalty to Fitzgerald. They stood
by him through the vicissitudes of his last years and lent him
money to help send Scottie through Vassar. When Fitzgerald paid
it back in full, Murphy wrote to him, characteristically, "I wish we
could feel we'd done you a service instead of making you feel some
kind of torment. Please dismiss the *thought*." Fitzgerald was
deeply grateful. In 1940, he wrote from Hollywood, "There was
many a day when the fact that you and Sara did help me . . . seemed

the only pleasant human thing that had happened in a world where I felt prematurely passed by and forgotten." They attended his funeral a few months later.

When the film version of *Tender Is the Night* came out in 1962, Gerald went to see it. Because Sara had flatly refused to go, Gerald went by himself, one Friday afternoon, to the local theater in Nyack where it was playing, and when he sat down he realized that there was no one else in the vast, darkened auditorium but an elderly charwoman sweeping the back rows. "It was an eerie sensation," he said, "and oddly appropriate somehow to the unreality of the film, which disregarded everything except the battle of the sexes and dismissed the lure of the era with a nostalgic ridiculing of the Charleston. It was so far from any sort of relationship to us, or the period, or poor Scott, that I couldn't feel any emotion at all except a vague sympathy for Jennifer Jones trying so hard to play the eighteen-year-old Nicole. I came out of the movie house and found that it had started to snow, so I went and had the chains put on the car. And then for some reason, driving home, I had a really vivid recollection of Scott on that day, years and years ago, when I gave him back the advance copy of his book and told him how good I thought certain parts of it were—not mentioning Sara's feelings—and Scott took the book and said, with that funny, faraway look in his eye, 'Yes, it has magic. It has magic.' "

TEN PAINTINGS

The ten paintings Gerald Murphy completed between the years 1922 and 1930 seem today, nearly half a century later, amazingly contemporary. Murphy's "American" response to the work of Picasso, Léger, and the other School of Paris modernists led him to a style that lay midway between realism and abstraction, and to an imagery that made use of commonplace objects presented in the bold manner and enlarged scale of commercial advertising. The emergence of a similar style and subject matter in the work of certain American Pop artists during the sixties was an important factor in the rediscovery of Murphy's work. Although they had been painted in a more optimistic era and in a different spirit, Murphy's pictures suddenly looked like fascinating precursors of Pop art.

Their rediscovery took place in 1960 when Douglas MacAgy, at the time director of the Dallas Museum for Contemporary Arts, exhibited half of Murphy's total *oeuvre* in a show called "American Genius in Review." MacAgy had learned of Murphy's paintings from Rudi Blesh, a writer on art, who had discussed them briefly in his book *Modern Art U.S.A.* MacAgy wrote to Murphy, who was retired by then from Mark Cross and living in Snedens Landing, New York, requesting permission to exhibit as many of his canvases as might be presently available. Surprised, somewhat dubious, yet undeniably pleased, Murphy agreed. Only five pictures were available, as it turned out. Four were from the Snedens Landing house (two of which were framed and hanging there, the other two rolled up in the attic); the fifth belonged to Archibald MacLeish. MacAgy showed them in Dallas in the spring of 1960, together with work by four other more-or-less forgotten Americans: Tom Benrimo, John Covert, Morgan Russell, and Morton L. Schamberg. The exhibition was the first public display of Murphy's work in America, and the first showing of it anywhere since 1936, when the Galerie Bernheim Jeune in Paris gave him a one-man show.

Meticulously composed and more subtle in color than the paintings of Stuart Davis, a contemporary whose work Murphy's somewhat resembles, the pictures today seem fresh, original, and full of authority. The Dallas showing and MacAgy's subsequent article about them in *Art in America* attracted widespread attention. Alfred H. Barr, Jr., who met Murphy in 1964, expressed serious interest in his work. "I think it is valuable aesthetically," he said. "I should like it to be exhibited in our museum, and I am deeply sorry that I had not known about it before." (Murphy's reaction to this, in a letter to a friend, was "*J'étais confus!*"). Soon afterward the Museum of Modern Art did acquire Murphy's *Wasp and Pear*, as a gift from Archibald MacLeish. Aware that Murphy was desperately ill with cancer, MacLeish telephoned René d'Harnoncourt, the museum's director, and told him that he would donate the painting if the museum would accept it quickly enough so that Gerald could be told at once. D'Harnoncourt acted immediately. When Murphy died that fall (1964), his *Wasp and Pear* was hanging in the Museum of Modern Art, alongside paintings by Léger and Picasso.

Although his teacher Natalia Goncharova refused to let him paint anything that bore the slightest resemblance to any real object or form, when Murphy began to work on his own he quickly found the balance between representation and abstraction that he would employ from then on. "Real objects which I admired had become for me abstractions, or objects in a world of abstraction," he told MacAgy. "My hope was to somehow digest them along with purely abstract forms and *re*-present them." There is a note of irony in his choice of subject matter for *Razor*, his first picture. While still employed at Mark Cross in 1915, Murphy was assigned by his father the task of developing an inexpensive safety razor. Mark Cross was on the verge of patenting the result when King C. Gillette unexpectedly came out with an almost identical product that swiftly captured the market. Gillette's razor, rampant on a field of safety matches and crossed with a couchant fountain pen, seems an apt symbol of Murphy's transmigration from commerce into art.

The influence of Léger is readily apparent in *Razor*. Murphy never studied with Léger, who was teaching then at the Atelier de la Grande Chaumière; but he and Sara used to visit his studio often, and Léger frequently took them off on excursions around Paris. "He talked constantly about the visual world, he saw and remarked everything, and he made you see it, too," Murphy once said. "One day he came to lunch at our apartment on the Quai des Grands-Augustins. Sara had put one rose in a tall vase on a shelf, against the white wall. Léger stopped short when he saw it. He pointed to the rose and exclaimed, 'The value of *that*!' Afterward he began using roses in his own pictures. He also used to say that painting was piracy, and that he was always picking up things from other artists.

"Once he took me into the railroad yards behind the Gare St. Lazare. The stationmaster knew him and let him go out into the yards, where there were miles and miles of track going in all directions. He wanted to show me the trainmen's signals. He was fascinated by them, by their design, shape, color, and contrast.

Razor, 32″ x 36″, 1922. Exhibited: Indépendants, 1923; Bernheim Jeune, 1936; Dallas Museum for Contemporary Arts, 1960. Collection of the Dallas Museum for Contemporary Arts.

'Nothing can be more powerful than those,' he said. 'They must be seen and recognized immediately.' He was so alive to everything visual, so determined to use the most powerful visual symbols in his pictures. He thought a painting should be an object in its own right, with the same force and presence that a natural or a machine-made object had. His dictum on abstract art has never been said better by anyone: 'You don't make a nail with a nail, but with iron.'"

Murphy had no desire to paint like the Paris artists who were his friends, and while his work shows Léger's influence, it is not derivative. He once wrote to MacAgy, "I feel that I was more influenced by what the good modern painters believed than by the way they painted."

Murphy had rented a studio in Montparnasse, one big room at 69, rue Froidevaux (Hemingway lived there for a few weeks in 1926, after he had separated from his first wife). In *Razor* he had painted small objects on a scale considerably larger than life-size. His second picture, which was eighteen feet tall, extended the idea to huge objects presented on a colossal scale, specifically, the smokestacks and ventilators of a Cunard ocean liner. This was the painting that Segonzac unsuccessfully tried to exclude from the 1924 Indépendants exhibition.

The problem of scale preoccupied Murphy in much the

Boatdeck, Cunarder, 18′ x 12′, 1923. Exhibited: Indépendants, 1924; Bernheim Jeune, 1936. The painting, which was rolled and stored by Bernheim Jeune, disappeared during the Second World War; attempts to trace it have so far failed.

Engine Room, 60" x 44", 1924. Exhibited: Indépendants, 1924; Bernheim Jeune, 1936. Whereabouts unknown.

Roulement à Billes, 60" x 40", 1926. Exhibited: Indépendants, 1926; Bernheim Jeune, 1936. Whereabouts unknown (no photo available).

same way it preoccupies Lichtenstein, Oldenburg, and other contemporary Pop artists. In a notebook that he used to jot down ideas for pictures, the following entry appears:

> Scene of a house interior with all chairs and furnishings done in colossal (or heroic) scale. People dwarfed climbing seriously into great chairs to talk to each other; struggling under the weight of huge pencil to write notes on square feet of paper: Man's good-natured tussle with the giant material world; or man's unconscious slavery to his material possessions.

One crucial difference between Murphy's work and Pop art can be seen in the attitude brought to bear on the problem of the material world. Today the tussle does not seem so good-natured; the slavery is no longer unconscious.

> *Always struck by the mystery and depth of the interior of a watch. Its multiplicity, variety and feeling of movement and man's grasp at perpetuity.*
> —GERALD MURPHY, Notebook

The twenties embraced the myth of the machine. Scorning the nineteenth century's aesthetic bias against industrialization, the futurist leader Marinetti had proclaimed in 1909 that a racing automobile was "more beautiful than the Victory of Samothrace," and Léger subsequently vowed to show "a bolt more beautiful than a rose." Three of Murphy's paintings dealt with machinery. *Engine*

Room, another aspect of the Cunarder whose stacks he had painted the year before, and *Roulement à Billes (Ball Bearing)*, inspired by a display of "S.K.F." Swedish ball bearings that he had seen in Paris, treated large industrial objects in purely formal terms. (Both paintings have since disappeared.) The six-foot-square, precisionist *Watch*, exhibited at the 1925 Indépendants, was more complex and more enigmatic. A rendering of small, familiar mechanical forms on a gigantic scale, the picture made a powerful impression on a number of other artists including Marcel Duchamp, several of whose paintings had depicted erotic acts as mechanical processes.

Cruising the Mediterranean on their sloop *Honoria*, the Murphys put into the harbor at Genoa one summer evening. They went ashore to buy provisions. In a small piazza facing the sea, just as the sun went down, Murphy saw an ancient chapel in the Ionic style, with white doves resting on its capitals and architraves: "I was struck by the relationship and took notes." The result was *Doves*, painted in the cool blue and gray tones of early Pompeian frescoes.

Architectural elements also dominate *Bibliothèque*, a painting based on Murphy's memory of objects in his father's library. Damaged while en route to the 1926 Indépendants, the picture was never exhibited. It now belongs to the Murphys' daughter.

Watch, 78″ x 78″, 1925. Exhibited: Indépendants, 1925; Bernheim Jeune, 1936; Dallas Museum for Contemporary Arts, 1960. Collection of the Dallas Museum for Contemporary Arts.

Doves, 47″ x 35″, 1925. Exhibited: Indépendants, 1925; Bernheim Jeune, 1936; Dallas Museum for Contemporary Arts, 1960. Collection of Honoria Donnelly.

Bibliothèque, 6′ x 4′, 1926. Collection of Honoria Donnelly (no photo available).

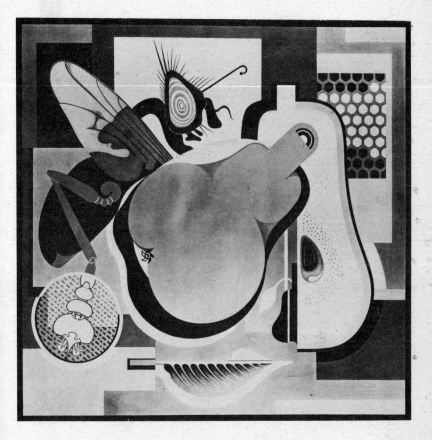

Wasp and Pear, 35″ x 37″, 1927. Exhibited: Bernheim Jeune, 1936; Dallas Museum for Contemporary Arts, 1960. Collection of the Museum of Modern Art.

> *Picture: hornet (colossal) on a pear (marks on skin, leaf veins, etc.) (battening on the fruit, clenched . . .)*
> —GERALD MURPHY, Notebook

In one of the letters he wrote to Sara before they were married in 1915, Murphy spoke of his fascination with winged insects. "Who knows," he joked, "some wretched insect which I save from your grinding heel may give you an inspired color for scarf or gown! Have you ever seen the lining of a potato bug's wings?" Many years later, Murphy remembered that while he was painting *Watch* and again in 1927 when he painted *Wasp and Pear*, he had been struck by the thought that perhaps these pictures expressed a kind of yearning for a native classicism "such as the Greeks must have craved . . . what Emerson meant when he wrote, 'And we [Americans] shall be classic *unto ourselves*.'" The rendering of particular natural details seen with absolute accuracy and as though for the first time, as Audubon saw them—to Murphy this seemed an American value.

An infinitely painstaking craftsman who never committed an idea to canvas until it had been thoroughly developed through countless preliminary sketches and *maquettes*, Murphy sometimes felt that his slow pace indicated a basic defect in his approach. It took him four months to finish painting the picture on the inside

Cocktail, 28″ x 29″, 1928. Exhibited: Bernheim Jeune, 1936; Dallas Museum for Contemporary Arts, 1960; North Carolina Museum of Art, 1961. Collection of Sara Murphy.

145

Portrait, 32″ x 32″, 1929–1930. Exhibited: Bernheim Jeune, 1936. Destroyed, 1944.

of the cigar box in *Cocktail* (an exact replica of the printed picture on a real cigar box; a Pop artist would do it more quickly with the aid of a silkscreen). Léger reassured him. "The Dutch and Flemish painters may have done the visual arts a disservice by inventing the use of oil in painting," Léger said. "Up to that time the various media—carving in stone and wood, mosaics, frescoes—were difficult, stiff, and uncompromising. No artist made a move indifferently. He dared not make a mistake. There was no canvas to scrape and just start over again."

Portrait, Gerald Murphy's last painting, includes an outline tracing of the artist's foot and its inked imprint, three Murphy thumb prints painted from original ink impressions (Murphy executed these with a brush from which he had extracted all but a single camel's hair), a magnified rendering of his eye, a twelve-inch ruler drawn to scale, and a painted copy of "the conglomerate standard facial profile of Caucasian Man from the archives of the Bibliothèque Nationale." The witty juxtaposition of images could be seen as a sardonic comment on Cubist "displacement." It also appeared to suggest a new direction in Murphy's painting, one that would never be developed. Before leaving Europe Murphy gave this painting to his friend Vladimir Orloff, the designer of the *Weatherbird*. It was destroyed during the war when American troops razed the cabin that Orloff was living in at Pampelonne, near St.-Tropez.

Asked once why he had stopped painting in 1930, Murphy replied that he had simply realized his work was not first-rate, "and the world was full of second-rate painting." Those closest to him found different explanations. Perhaps the attempt to make one's own life into a work of art becomes, in the end, inimical to serious work in any field: "Either a comfortable life and lousy work or a lousy life and beautiful work," Léger once remarked. Living well, however, was not a sufficiently adequate revenge for Murphy. He once told a friend that he had never been entirely happy until he began painting, and that he was never really happy again after he stopped.